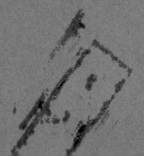

Walt Whitman's Camden Conversations

Walt Whitman by Thomas Eakins, painted from life, oil on canvas, 30 x 24. The Pennsylvania Academy of the Fine Arts

Walt Whitman's Camden Conversations

Selected and arranged with
an introduction by

WALTER TELLER

RUTGERS UNIVERSITY PRESS
New Brunswick, New Jersey

Library of Congress Cataloging in Publication Data

Whitman, Walt, 1819–1892.
    Walt Whitman's Camden conversations.

    Selections from With Walt Whitman in Camden, by H. Traubel.
    I. Teller, Walter Magnes, 1910–   ed.
II. Traubel, Horace, 1858–1919. With Walt Whitman in Camden.
1973. III. Title.
PS3222.W3   1973   811'.3   73–8509
ISBN   0–8135–0767–7

Failing to fetch me at first keep encouraged,
Missing me one place search another . . .

Whitman, "Song of Myself"

OTHER BOOKS BY WALTER TELLER

The Farm Primer, 1941
Roots in the Earth (with P. Alston Waring), 1943
An Island Summer, 1951
The Search for Captain Slocum: A Biography, 1956
The Voyages of Joshua Slocum, 1958
Five Sea Captains, 1960
Area Code 215: A Private Line in Bucks County, 1963
Cape Cod and the Offshore Islands, 1970
Joshua Slocum, 1971
Twelve Works of Naïve Genius, 1972

CONTENTS

ILLUSTRATIONS

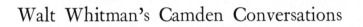

Walt Whitman's Camden Conversations

Mickle Street. Whitman's house is the small one on the right. From *Visits to Walt Whitman in 1890–1891* by J. Johnston, M.D., and J. W. Wallace

SETTING

The Walt Whitman House on Mickle Street, Camden, owned and looked after by the State of New Jersey, captures the time and scene of this book. Though the neighborhood has been wiped out since Whitman's day—scarcely another dwelling on either side of the street remains and even the street itself is almost obliterated—the house and its furnishings are about as they were when he lived there during the 1880s and early 1890s. A low-lying, gray clapboard, two-story row house, it filled a slot between brick houses three stories high that are no longer there; the Whitman house, a historic site now, survives alone. It is open to visitors.

From a low-slung stoop you enter a narrow hall. On the left is the parlor, ahead and to the rear lies the kitchen, and to the right, against the wall, a narrow stairway leads to the second floor where Whitman, invalided, spent his last years. Upstairs, the simple pieces of furniture stand where they stood when he was alive; his table and broad-beamed chair in front of one of the windows, his outsize wood-framed bed by the west wall, and opposite it, a hard horse-hair sofa. Most of the conversations that follow took place in this room. When talking with Horace Traubel, his friend and constant visitor, Whitman would often rest on the bed while Traubel usually sat on the sofa.

Many photographs were taken of Whitman, and some of Traubel, but I have not seen a picture of them together. They must have presented a lively contrast. Whitman was turning seventy but he looked older. Six feet tall, weighing 200 pounds, he had quiet gray eyes, and his white hair and beard were long and flowing. Horace Traubel, thirty years old, narrow-shouldered and short, had bright blue eyes and a shock of thick, wavy light-brown hair. A mustache did not hide his boyish appearance. While Whitman spoke and Traubel listened, Traubel was also writing, swiftly and unobtrusively.

For four years Traubel visited Whitman daily, sometimes two or three times a day—almost never missed—and day after day he took down in what he called "condensed longhand" whatever Whitman said. "Within the hour of the words spoken," he put the notes, written on small sheets of paper in double columns, into the form in which he published them. In 1906, fourteen years after Whitman's death, he brought out the first volume of *With Walt Whitman in Camden,* the chronological record of those visits interspersed with reams of other data—mostly old letters—that Whitman had given him. Four volumes followed, a total of 2,600 pages.

"I have let Whitman alone," Traubel wrote in his introduction to volume one. "This book is more his book than my book. It talks his words. It reflects his manner." A contemporary of Traubel's, Harrison Morris, who called on Whitman a number of times, wrote, "Horace has caught the very accent of Walt's voice. . . . he grew so skilled in Walt's vocabulary, oddness of phrase, and course of thought that he could finish a sentence once begun, as Whitman would do it himself. . . . I can detect the phrase and modulation of Walt's slow, hesitating and sonorous speech on every page of Traubel's . . . imperishable files."

Though Whitman's impromptu remarks must be among the best ever recorded, they have all but dropped out of sight; very few persons have plowed through Traubel's massive compilation. With the permission of his daughter, Gertrude Traubel, I excerpted what seem Whitman's finest

Horace Traubel, age 35

comments and arranged them under headings listed alpha-
betically in order to make Whitman's spoken expression
easily available and in compact form. Sifting through *With
Walt Whitman in Camden,* I chose what I liked, gathered
only what appealed to me.

"Camden was originally an accident—but I shall never
be sorry I was left over in Camden! It has brought me
blessed returns," Whitman told Traubel. Born 31 May
1819 at West Hills, Long Island, of English, Dutch and
Welsh stock, Walt was the second of the nine children of
Walter and Louisa Van Velsor Whitman. He attended
public school in Brooklyn until he was twelve or so, worked
as an office boy, printer's apprentice, and for a time, begin-
ning at age seventeen, taught school in the rural districts
of Long Island. He wrote for various Long Island newspapers, started one of his own, and edited successively ten
or more Brooklyn and New York papers. In 1848 he went
south to take a newspaper job in New Orleans but after a
few months returned to Brooklyn, where he continued to
edit, write, and to some extent follow his father's trade of
carpenter. In 1855, when he was thirty-six, he published his
first edition of *Leaves of Grass,* twelve untitled poems including "Song of Myself." The following year he produced
an expanded edition and in 1860 still another.

The Civil War began. In 1862, hearing his brother
George, an officer in the Union Army, had been wounded,
Walt went to Washington to find out about him; from there
he went to an army camp in Virginia, where he remained
until George recovered. Returning to Washington, Walt
stayed on, volunteering as a kind of social worker in army
hospitals while employed as a government clerk, first in the
Department of the Interior and then in the Attorney
General's Office. He made lasting friendships, especially

with William Douglas O'Connor and his wife Nellie and
John Burroughs. And he wrote his Civil War poems, including "When Lilacs Last in the Dooryard Bloom'd,"
brought out revised and enlarged editions of *Leaves of
Grass,* a selected edition in England, and published a prose
pamphlet, *Democratic Vistas.* Then early in 1873, age 53,
he suffered a stroke.

Partly paralyzed and disabled, Whitman left the capital
and headed for Camden, on the Delaware River, opposite
Philadelphia, where his brother George, mustered out when
the war ended, worked as a pipe tester and inspector.
George and his wife Louisa took Walt into their home, a
temporary arrangement that lasted the better part of the
next ten years.

Though not as yet widely honored, neither was Whitman
unknown. Soon after Walt's unexpected appearance at
George's house on Stevens Street, Maurice Henry Traubel,
an engraver and lithographer living around the corner, called
to pay respects to the poet newly arrived in town. Born in
Germany of Jewish parents, Maurice Traubel had come to
America as a young man, married an American Methodist,
Katherine Grunder, and launched a family. Horace, the
fifth of Maurice and Katherine Traubel's seven children,
was born in Camden, 19 December 1858.

Reminiscing years later Whitman said, "Horace, you
were a mere boy then: we met—don't you remember? . . .
I remember you so well: you were so slim, so upright, so
sort of electrically buoyant. You were like medicine to me—
better than medicine . . . down on Stevens Street, out front
there, under the trees. You would come along, I would be
sitting there: we would have our chats. Oh! you were reading then like a fiend: you were always telling me about your
endless books, books. . . ."

"One of my first memories of the old man . . . was

sitting with him under the trees in front of the house of a mild summer evening, he on a chair and I on the curb," Horace Traubel wrote long afterward. "I don't know whether he liked me or not. But he invariably welcomed me. 'Howdy—howdy!' "

Traubel's schooling and early jobs were not unlike Whitman's. After quitting the classroom at age twelve, he tended a newspaper route, ran errands, helped his father, who kept a stationery store, and worked as a printer's devil for a Camden printery. He set type, read proof, wrote editorials, and did reporting for the *Camden Evening Visitor*. He was also a lithographer and for a time held a job as a factory paymaster. Early in life he decided he wanted to write. He said to Whitman, "I used to regret that I missed going to college."

"You regret it no longer?"

"I see now that I was in luck."

"Good for you: you were in luck: you made a providential escape: for a fellow with your rebel independence, with your ability to take care of yourself, with your almost nasty resolution to go your own road, a college is not necessary— would in fact be a monster mountain of obstruction. As between a university course anyhow and a struggle of the right sort in the quick of everyday life the life course would beat the university course every time."

In 1884, with earnings from a spurt in the sale of *Leaves of Grass* and a loan from a well-wisher, Whitman bought the house at 328 Mickle Street, a "plain little abode in a shabby street," as one visitor then described it, only a block from the railroad yard, where freight trains were constantly shunting and banging. Soon after moving in he became acquainted with a neighbor, Mary Oakes Davis, a helpful, warm-hearted, forty-seven-year-old widow. Mrs. Davis was paying rent for her premises. Whitman proposed

Another view of Whitman's house, Mary Davis at the door. Photograph by J. Johnston, M.D.

that she share his house rent free in return for furnishing it; she had furniture and household goods while he had virtually nothing. Early the following year Mrs. Davis moved in and from then on, in Whitman's words, was his "housekeeper, nurse and friend."

Another friend, Thomas Donaldson, wrote that Whitman could have found a better house for less money; he had paid $1,750 cash. "I think that the fact that there was a tree in front of it, that it was convenient to the ferries, and that lilacs grew in the back yard, determined Mr. Whitman to buy it. . . . The . . . house . . . was cramped and full of cracks. It contained no furnace, and his bedroom ceiling could be easily touched with the hand. He enjoyed it nevertheless. It was situated in a commercial part of Camden. . . . there was certainly the vilest odor, at times. . . . It came from a guano factory on the Philadelphia side of the Delaware River." Richard Maurice Bucke, M.D., Whitman's friend, correspondent, and first biographer called it, "The worst house and the worst situated."

The northeast was still digging out of the most famous blizzard in American history, Edison was perfecting the cylinder phonograph, and Grover Cleveland, the first Democrat in the White House since pre-Civil War days, was far along in his first term as President when Horace Traubel began his daily visits to Mickle Street, 28 March 1888. By this time he was courting his future wife, Anne Montgomerie. He told her of his visits with Whitman and repeated to her some things the poet said. She urged him to write down everything—so Horace and Anne's daughter, Gertrude, informed me when I went to see her. During the years that Traubel called every day, he helped Whitman publish new work and reissue old. And he also did more—a great deal more—ministering in countless ways to the old poet's ease and comfort. He bought a woodburning stove for Whitman's bedroom, selected a wheelchair when it became necessary, wrote letters, paid bills, handled orders for books, arranged interviews, answered inquiries about Whitman, and served as informal treasurer for a group of his friends who contributed to the cost of the male nurse and other expenses. On one occasion, acting as courier, Traubel traveled to Washington carrying messages between Whitman and his dying friend, William Douglas O'Connor.

Traubel usually arrived in the evening. Eight, he noticed was Whitman's "good hour invariably if there is a good hour. . . . ." After two months of constant attendance—by which time a routine must have seemed established—he wrote, "W. was very affectionate in his manner tonight. 'Come here, Horace,' he said. I went over. He took my hand. 'I feel somehow as if you had consecrated yourself to me. That entails something on my part: I feel somehow as if I was consecrated to you. Well—we will work out the rest of my life-job together: it won't be for long: anyway, we'll work it out together, for short or long, eh?' He took my face between his hands and drew me to him and kissed me. Nothing more was said. I went back to my chair and we sat in silence for some time."

On a spring morning Traubel described Whitman's second floor room. "There are three windows, all opening north . . . ." Traubel wrote. "The west window is rarely opened—not even curtain thrown up—except in warmest weather. Between this and the center window against the wall is a big round table. It is on this table he eats his meals, facing west, and it is the center window by which he sits when not doing anything. The third window (the east) has his big square table nearly against it; and this with a box underneath, and chairs about him, is the repository of his working materials. When working he wheels from his window, his left side against the square table, his back towards the light. Takes a pad on his knee—always writes that way. The east window he will sometimes raise, and fix the blinds for light, but his main dependence is always on the center window. He never throws the shutters open. The blinds he will put at the down-angle if he wishes to look into the street, and at the horizontal or up, if simply studying the sky, or ruminating."

Another evening Traubel wrote, "The strange medley in the room: I looked it over some: veritably a work room: here in the lowered light with W. so sick in his bed and the book stuff about him in this inexplicable way: it affected me profoundly."

Mrs. Davis, who kept house for Whitman and waited on him, saw the room in a different light. "Mary thinks it an utterly indecent place—disorder added to disorder," Whitman remarked while Traubel was searching for something mislaid among the papers on Whitman's table. "This room is full of lost and found," the old man said, laughing. A letter yellow with age that Traubel happened on had, in Whitman's words, "floated up and down on the tides of this room for six years or so." Finally Mary Davis, helped by one Mrs. Mapes, and with Traubel lending a hand, insisted on cleaning up. "We even found stuff under the carpet," Traubel wrote, "letters, sheets of written-over paper. God knows how they got there. The merely worthless paper was shoved into the stove. The letters, &c., were put into a big washbasket. In one corner we came upon a baby's shoe. We found a bunch of good postage stamps all stuck together— about three dollars' worth of one's and two's."

"Mrs. Mapes has an enlarged bump of order," Whitman said when it was over. "She arranged my things so I didn't know where a damn thing was: her heart is in the right place, though she has put everything . . . in the wrong

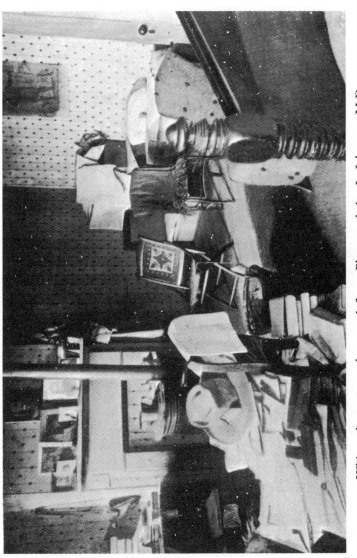

Whitman's room on the second floor. Photograph by J. Johnston, M.D.

place." *Status quo ante bellum* was soon restored, however, and Traubel could write, "The work corner . . . is now as bad as ever. Things are weltered all about." One time Traubel picked up a sheet of scorched manuscript. It seems that after Whitman had turned in for the night, Ed Wilkins, the nurse, had gone into his room, noticed smoke, and then "discovered that . . . papers . . . pushed against the stove . . . were smouldering." Traubel wrote there were several such incidents.

Whitman had never depended on publishers. He had set some of the type for the first edition of *Leaves of Grass,* read and corrected proof himself, and ordered the binding. In his final years, with day-to-day help from Traubel, he brought out *November Boughs,* with the preface, "A Backward Glance O'er Travel'd Roads," the poems he called "Sands at Seventy," *Complete Poems and Prose 1855–1888,* a pocket-size *Leaves of Grass* in time for his seventieth birthday, reprints of several early editions and the last, the so termed deathbed edition. Traubel acted as Whitman's agent with George S. Ferguson, a printer in Philadelphia; he carried Whitman's copy across the river, then returned to Camden with estimates, specifications, and proofs. He took instructions to Frederick Oldach, the binder, also in Philadelphia, and in due course delivered the finished books to Whitman. "Of all the people I have known or know," Whitman told him, "you are the most fitted to help me just now. You know books, writers, printing office customs—best of all you know *me*—my ways and what I need to be humored in."

Traubel wrote in November 1888, "W. was rather cranky tonight. Jumped on me for not having some message from Ferguson. 'What the hell?' he asked two or three times. I got tired of hearing it and asked him: 'What the hell?' too.

That made him laugh. I said: 'If I'm doing so miserable bad why don't you bounce me?' He looked indignant for a minute: then said: 'I couldn't: you wouldn't be bounced.' 'Then you'd better accept me the way I am.' I was a bit mad myself. We don't have many tiffs. Finally he said: 'Don't let's go on in that vein. . . .' "

As they continued working together Whitman offered to share what money he had with Traubel, but Traubel said no, they would not be bound by money arrangements. Whitman called their understanding a solemn pact ratified by love. "To *Horace Traubel* from his friend the author Walt Whitman," he wrote in a copy of *Complete Poems and Prose,* "& my deepest heartfelt thanks go with it to H T in getting this book out—it is *his* book in a sense—for I have been closely imprison'd & prostrated all the time (June to December 1888) by sickness & disability—& H T has managed it all for me with copy, proofs, printing, binding, &c. The Volume, & especially 'November Boughs' & the portraits, could not now be existing formulated as here, except thro' his faithful & loving kindness & industry, daily, unintermitted, unremunerated—W W Dec: 1888—Camden New Jersey—"

In March 1889, Traubel wrote, "W. asked me to see Oldach again. 'Try to stir him up: tell him we want our book. My God! but he's a time-taker: he's slower'n pitch on a frosty morning! That book has been there about a month: it should be done: what must we do to get it? Go there: don't hurt him: ram a needle in his ass—not too far: not far enough to hurt him—only far enough to wake him up.' He was so funny about this I burst into a furious laugh. This broke him loose too, and he haha'd till the tears flowed down his cheeks like rain."

Knowing that Traubel intended to write about him, Whitman gave him all manner of documents for what he called Traubel's "archives." When handing over—bidding good-bye—to old letters, he usually asked Traubel to read them aloud. " 'Horace, I've got a job for you: I want you to read me these letters.' He handed me sheets of paper pinned together. They were old and soiled. . . . An O'Connor letter first. Then a [John] Burroughs letter. Then another letter from O'Connor. He settled comfortably in a chair. I read. . . . W. was enthusiastic by the time I got through. He interrupted me throughout with exclamations and comments. He had me read some passages a second time. Broke right in and said: 'Go back a bit—read that again.' "

Whitman lived to see his work published in half a dozen languages. A stream of visitors came to Mickle Street, persons of all degrees; radicals and the well-to-do, writers, professors of literature, denizens of the neighborhood, and quite a few from abroad. "Went down with Tom Harned," Traubel noted on a spring evening. "W. sitting in front of the house, his chair drawn next the step. A couple of boys, quite small ones, lounging there with him. . . . W. greeted us heartily, two or three flowers in one hand, his glasses in the other, the inevitable cane blocked up between the knees. People came up and shook hands with him, now one, now another."

While serving Whitman and working for him, Traubel was also making a living and taking part in community life; he was active in the Contemporary Club, which he organized in 1886. In 1889 he got a job in a bank and the following year, while continuing at the bank, inaugurated a monthly paper, *The Conservator,* published in Philadelphia. It provided him with a forum wherein he could have his say about society, religion, politics, literature, and art; and it also enabled him to publish scores of articles on Whitman by himself and others. Resigning from the bank in 1902, he managed thereafter on what he was able to earn as editor and publisher of *The Conservator,* and as a free lance journalist. He brought out two volumes of verse, *Chants Communal,* 1904, *Optimos,* 1910, and a volume of prose pieces, *Collects,* 1914; he directed a short-lived monthly, *The Artsman,* and as one of Whitman's literary executors (with Bucke and Harned) edited several books by or about him in addition to *With Walt Whitman in Camden.* The last issue of *The Conservator* appeared in June 1919. The following 8 September, in his sixty-first year, Traubel died and was buried in Harleigh Cemetery, Camden, not far from Whitman's tomb.

Three volumes of *With Walt Whitman in Camden* appeared in Traubel's lifetime, two posthumously. Small, Maynard & Company published the first, D. Appleton and Company the second in 1908, and Mitchell Kennerley the third in 1914. Traubel had prepared a typescript of volume four but was unable to find a publisher. Almost forty years later, in 1953, the University of Pennsylvania Press brought it out. Volume five came from Southern Illinois University Press in 1965, edited by Gertrude Traubel. Traubel's fifth volume ends with his entry for 14 September 1889, when two and a half years still remained to Whitman. The rest of his notes have not been published.

When I first considered selecting the best of Whitman from Traubel's pages, I asked Betty Vas Nunes Burroughs to work with me. From start to finish she did yeoman service.

Long ago my father, Chester Jacob Teller, gave me his Whitman collection including the first three volumes of *With Walt Whitman in Camden.* Witting or unwitting, he laid the groundwork.

Gertrude Traubel authorized the use of copyright material. Talking with her brought the Whitman circle very close—her parents were married in Whitman's house with Whitman present; she was almost a link with Whitman himself. "Papa told me I was at Whitman's funeral but didn't know it," she said when I visited her in Germantown, Philadelphia, in February 1972. She was born in April 1892; Whitman died 26 March, three weeks earlier.

A note. Everything in the following chapters (unless marked otherwise) comes from *With Walt Whitman in Camden.* Each item is identified by date: March 28–July 14, 1888, Vol. I; July 16–October 31, 1888, Vol. II; November 1, 1888–January 20, 1889, Vol. III; January 21–April 7, 1889, Vol. IV; April 8–September 14, 1889, Vol. V. I kept to Traubel's punctuation, capitalization and spelling—left things as they were, observed the original and, I hope, retained the flavor.

W. T.
Princeton, New Jersey
Spring 1973

SOURCES OF PRECEDING QUOTATIONS

Abbreviation: WWWC stands for Traubel's *With Walt Whitman in Camden.*

"condensed longhand" WWWC, IV.x
"I have . . . his manner." WWWC, I.viii
"within the . . . words spoken" WWWC, V. Editor's Preface

"Horace has . . . imperishable files." Harrison S. Morris, *Walt Whitman* (Cambridge, Mass., 1929), p. 96

"Camden was . . . blessed returns." WWWC, II.29

"Horace, you . . . books, books" WWWC, III.407

"One of . . . Howdy—howdy" "The Conservator" (Philadelphia, March 1919), p. 2

"I used . . . every time." WWWC, II.468–69

"plain little . . . shabby street" Morris, *Whitman,* p. 77

"housekeeper, nurse and friend." Elizabeth Leavitt Keller, *Walt Whitman in Mickle Street* (New York, 1921), p. 21

"I think . . . Delaware River." Thomas Donaldson, *Walt Whitman the Man* (New York, 1896), pp. 66–67

"The worst . . . worst situated." WWWC, V.181

"good hour . . . good hour" WWWC, III.194

"W. was . . . some time." WWWC, I.207

"There are . . . or ruminating." WWWC, V.80

"The strange . . . me profoundly." WWWC, III.280

"Mary thinks . . . to disorder" WWWC, I.412

"This room . . . and found" Ibid.

"floated up . . . or so" WWWC, IV.509

"We even . . . and two's." WWWC, IV.467

"Mrs. Mapes . . . wrong place." WWWC, IV.448

"The work . . . all about." WWWC, IV.510–11

"discovered that . . . were smouldering." WWWC, III.257

"Of all . . . humored in." WWWC, I.187

"W. was . . . that vein" WWWC, III.177–78

"To Horace . . . New Jersey—" WWWC, III.363

"W. asked . . . like rain." WWWC, IV.282–83

"archives" WWWC, I.66

" 'Horace, I've . . . that again." WWWC, III.349,352

"Went down . . . now another." WWWC, V.191

Walt Whitman, age 35. Engraving by Sam'l Hollyer. Used in 1855
Leaves of Grass. The Historical Society of Pennsylvania

ACTORS & SPEAKERS

7.45 P.M. W. sitting up. In pretty good condition. Reading and writing some today. . . . Gave him The Stage. He took it gratefully. "I can say of this that it is the only paper on the list that I read right through, top to toe." . . .

W. asked then: "Did you ever come much in contact with actors?" I had not. . . . "I have always had a good deal to do with actors: met many, high and low: they are gassy: you'll have to beware of that, to take no account of that: but after that is said, there is more, and more important, to their credit. I have always had one question for actors: a question they have never answered, however: I put it to them this way: How is it that whatever the conditions— sick, worried, fagged out, grumpy—they can turn their backs on the common life, away from distractions, and engage in the new rôle at once: everything thrown off but the tragedy, comedy, whatnot of the moment. . . . I suppose that's the art: that's the secret of the profession."

January 12, 1889

These actor people always make themselves at home with me and always make me easily at home with them. I feel rather close to them—very close—almost like one of their kind. When I was much younger—way back: in the Brooklyn days—and even behind Brooklyn—I was to be an orator—to go about the country spouting my pieces, proclaiming my faith. I trained for all that—spouted in the woods, down by the shore, in the noise of Broadway where nobody could hear me: spouted, eternally spouted, and spouted again. I thought I had something to say—I was afraid I would get no chance to say it through books: so I was to lecture and get myself delivered that way. I think I had a good voice: I think I was never afraid—I had no stage reticences (I tried the thing often enough to see that.) For awhile I speechified in politics, but that, of course, would not satisfy me—that at the best was only come-day go-day palaver: what I really had to give out was something more serious, more off from politics and towards the general life.

March 30, 1888

I was a great spouter in my early days—even later on— had my favorite pieces. . . . "A Voice Out of the Sea," my own piece was one—one of many. I always enjoyed saying it—saying it to the winds, the waters, the noisy streets— on stagecoaches. And one has love for the sound of his own voice—somehow it's always magnetic.

August 27, 1889

I am particularly susceptible to voices: voices of range, magnetism: mellow, persuading voices. [J. Leonard] Corning hadn't much intrinsically to say, but his voice was worth while.

May 5, 1888

. . . take the bull by the horns at the start: discard the notes—go on your own hook: it cannot be discovered too soon that this is the only real public speaking—the speaking without a barrier.

December 8, 1888

A lecturer, writer, poet, talker, anybody, carries with him his aura or not—his assurance of success—a quality most real, but wholly indefinable.

May 2, 1889

ADVICE

In with W. Harned already there. W. in excellent good humor, feeling much better than yesterday, his face ruddy again, his hand warm. Sat by the window, in the parlor, in one of the armchairs. Chatted freely, with vigor and expressive gesture. Not out today—weather too uncertain. . . . "Horace, take my advice: never take advice!" Breaking out into merry laughter: "That sounds like a bull, Horace, but it's damned serious. No man who's got anything to do in the world can afford to take advice."

May 14, 1888

When you write do you take anybody's advice about writing? Don't do it: nothing will so mix you up as advice. If a fellow wants to keep clear about himself he must first of all swear a big oath that he'll never take any advice.

April 19, 1888

Advice forces its way into the temple—it don't belong there.

June 15, 1888

I am always telling you not to take advice. I mean it—every word of it: but that don't mean you are not to advise yourself or take your own advice.

May 27, 1888

One advantage a thing has if a man disregards the advice of his friends—it is all his own—an expression purely of his own personality: free of blemishes nothing could be, but freedom from alien influences: ah! that is necessary.

November 18, 1888

To vary the monotony of my life I received a long letter of advice . . . from a preacher up in Maine who said if I wrote more like other people and less like myself other people would like me better. I have no doubt they would. But where would Walt Whitman come in on that deal?

May 13, 1888

My friends, some of them, the more conservative of them (wishing me well as they did), were always saying to others, to me, in print, vocally, that *if* I would only tame myself a little I might, and so forth and so forth.

April 6, 1889

I am pursued, pursued, by advisers—advisers. They love me, they hate me—but they advise, advise! What would become of me if I listened to them? I am deaf to them all—deaf—deaf. The more they yell, the deafer I become. Why, I never move a step, write a word, that somebody don't object to: the thing that one likes another don't—the thing another likes one don't: it is God bless you for this or that, or God damn you for this or that. A fellow might easily be lost in the confusion: he's got no business to hear any of it: he's to hear only himself—that's his whole concern.

May 18, 1888

It's queer how the advisers spring up everywhere like mushrooms. I used to think God was everywhere. I was wrong: the adviser is everywhere!

May 21, 1888

AGE

Evening. W's day miserable. . . . Was up only about ten minutes this evening, though he talked from the bed in an easy, cheery way. I handed him some proofs. He was happy over it. "This looks like getting on the move again" —asking me: "Does Ferguson make any comments on my snail-like method of work?" Osler was over today. Says: "Do not take a gloomy view of Whitman's case—he will come around." . . . Some one set some fire crackers off right under his window. W. said of it: "Don't that beat the devil? Mary [Davis] wanted to go out today and raise a racket about the firing, but I would not let her. I would rather have a headache than interfere with the boys." . . . Hobbled about the room. "This cane was given me by Pete Doyle," he reminded me. . . . From his bed he cried to me: "How sweet the bed—the dear bed! When a fellow is physically in the dumps the bed gives him a sort of freedom."

July 3, 1888

....

I am getting more and more satisfied with my bed and chair, which is suspicious.

May 24, 1888

I am of course only gradually though surely losing strength, but the experiences going with this do not disturb me. . . . I am convinced that I can feint off the end for a long time to come. . . . we must stick, eternally stick, until sticking itself will stick no more.

April 3, 1888

Visitors are so severe a strain, every one seems like half a dozen. It is an ominous fact that I cannot stand visitors— the most ominous fact of all—because visitors, friends, lovers, comrades, whatever, are the last things I want to give up. But what can I do with this constant lethargy, lan- guidness, drowsiness, (tendency to sleep when I do not sleep) hanging over me? Sometimes I seem sentenced to death: everything but the date is fixed.

June 15, 1888

No doubt I got on the nether side of fate for a day or two but—well, here I am, dying, perhaps, as The Herald says, but not dead.

June 12, 1888

I have always had an idea that I should some day move off—be alone: finish my life in isolation: it may not seem just like me to say that, but I've felt so: at the last, after my fires were spent. For the most part I have desired to remain in the midst of the hurly-burly—to be where the crowd is: to make use of its magnetism, to borrow life from its magnetism: my heart is always with the people, in the thick of the struggle.

December 28, 1888

. . . I was a great deal more vehement years ago than I am now—Oh! I know I was! In my old days I take on the usual privilege of years—to go slow, to be less vehement, to trust more to quiet, to composure.

August 1, 1889

It's fine to see the green again. I wonder how many more springs I will last? Not many, I guess. You should see the wheat—wheat, wheat, everywhere. How tired, how good, I feel! Very tired, O very—but not sick. The sweet sun has got into all my old bones.

May 6, 1888

I never get entirely down in the mouth—I do not seem to have any scare in me—but I am wide awake to the fact of my gathering physical disabilities. It don't take an expert weather prophet to see some storms coming.

May 21, 1888

More and more as I grow old do I see the futility of calculation: refuse myself illusions—try not to get into the habit of expecting certain things at certain times—of planning for tomorrows, the eternal tomorrows, that never come quite as we arrange for them.

June 13, 1888

···

AMBITION

···

"What a sweat I used to be in all the time," said W., "over getting my damned books published! When I look back at it I wonder I didn't somewhere or other on the road chuck the whole business into oblivion. Editions! Editions! Editions! like the last extra of a newspaper: an extra after an extra: one issue after another: fifty-five, fifty-six, sixty-one, sixty-seven—oh! edition after edition. Yes, I wonder I never did anything violent with the book, it has so victimized me!" I broke into a broad "Ha! ha!" He lifted his head—leaned on his elbow. "What the hell! What are you breaking loose about now?" "Oh! I was only thinking how the poor victim is still making edition after edition: now, even, in eighty-eight—thirty-three years after fifty-five." [1855, first edition of *Leaves of Grass*] W. chuckled over this too. "It does seem rather laughable, don't it? But the fact is, the bug bites: we can't help ourselves: we are in a web—we are moths in flames: all of us: you, too, damn you! you'll have your bug some day: then maybe you'll have some sympathy for me!"

January 18, 1889

················

Back of the whole business, of course, is a precedent fact —the world don't need the book anyhow. But one man has the presidential bee in his bonnet—another has the book bee there: I have the book bee.

May 25, 1888

. . . I have had ambitions: no one is without ambition: nothing can be done without it: but I had no notion of simply shining—of doing something brilliant, showy, to catch the popular imagination: I can say I never was bitten by that poisonous bug: but . . . there were some things I wanted to do—some things I wanted to say: I was very eager to get my life according to a certain plan—to get my book written so, according to a certain plan: I was very resolute about that: that was my ambition: to get certain things said and done.

December 18, 1888

The work on the book does me good—stimulates me— bears me up. I think I should die if I didn't have the book to do. It is necessary to have an ambition—purpose—something you must absolutely, personally, do.

July 10, 1888

It's the finest thing in the world to be able to do justice to some study—do it whole justice—not exactly exhaust it (that is impossible) but to treat it with a sort of final comprehensiveness, dignity.

August 28, 1888

I have never had, nor have, any wish to make a big flareup: a big flare-up is soon out. I am aware that my work, if it has any stuff in it—any substance that can endure—needs time to make its way, and if it has not is as well dropped now as later.

September 4, 1888

AMERICA

W. spoke of material successes in civilization. "What do they show? Not necessarily much: we make a big noise about the things we have done, accumulated—what we can do and will do: with some of this I have some sympathy: but after all the main question is, what is all this doing for the men, women, children of America? The goods are worthless alone: they might demonstrate failure as well as success. Do you think goods can succeed and men can fail? They must succeed or fail together—they are damned or saved together."

May 7, 1888

. . . American life—every man is trying to outdo every other man—giving up modesty, giving up honesty, giving up generosity, to do it: creating a war, every man against every man: the whole wretched business falsely keyed by money ideals, money politics, money religions, money men.

April 16, 1888

God help our liberties when money has finally got our institutions in its clutch.

July 21, 1888

I know nothing more miserable, sickening, than Will it pay? as it is usually asked.

September 6, 1888

The trouble here with us is our devil of a craze for money —money in everything for every occasion—by hook or by crook, money: and, on top of that, show, show: crowning all that, brilliancy, smartness unsurpassed, repartee, social wish-wash, very misleading, very superficial: the whole situation one to discourage the more efficient factors of character.

August 23, 1888

Go on, my dear Americans, whip your horses to the utmost—Excitement; money! politics!—open all your valves and let her go—going, whirl with the rest—you will soon get under such momentum you can't stop if you would. Only make provision betimes, old States and new States, for several thousand insane asylums. You are in a fair way to create a nation of lunatics.

April 10, 1888

We are growing: this present mad rush for money—every man robbing from every man—cannot last. Our American people after all have enough sense to revise themselves when there is need for it. . . . I don't expect an upset—I expect a growth: evolution.

May 27, 1888

It is said reproachfully of America that she is material, but that to me is her glory—the body must precede the soul: the body is the other side of the soul.

May 6, 1888

While I seem to love America, and wish to see America prosperous, I do not seem able to bring myself to love America, to desire American prosperity, at the expense of some other nation or even of all other nations.

April 1, 1888

The spirit of the tariff is malevolent: it flies in the face of all American ideals: I hate it root and branch: it helps a few rich men to get rich, it helps the great mass of poor men to get poorer: what else does it do? . . . It is a robber age: the maxim of the law is, rob or be robbed. Of all robbers I think the tariff is the meanest robber. It has such sneaky, sneaking ways: it hits you in the back—hits you when you ain't lookin': gives you no sort of chance to protect yourself.

May 4, 1888

Protectionism, one nation against another nation, property all of it in a few hands, none of it in the many hands—such things, conditions, ask questions which America must answer—yes, answer in the right voice, with the right decision (answer for democracy's sake) or leave our republic to go to hell for its pains.

September 12, 1888

I am for free trade because I am for anything which will break down barriers between peoples: I want to see the countries all wide open.

May 13, 1888

Whitman about 43 years old. Photograph by Mathew B. Brady

If America is not for freedom I do not see what it is for. We ought to invite the world through an open door—all men—yes, even the criminals—giving to everyone a chance —a new outlook. My God! are men always to go on clawing each other—always to go on taxing, stealing, warring, having a class to exclude and a class excluded—always to go on having favorite races, favorite castes—a few people with money here and there—all the rest without anything everywhere?

May 4, 1888

We are often asked: Why should we do anything to help the English, the German, the Hungarian workman? Why should we? Why *shouldn't* we? It looks as good one way to me as another. I am not ashamed to confess that I am willing to have the foreign workman live. Home industry! Whose home? What home? I am not slow to say—am not afraid to say—I consider men en masse—for benefits as well as for other things.

September 13, 1888

I must insist upon the masses . . . their integrity as a whole—not, of course, denying or excusing what is bad. . . . it is good, not bad, that is common. The older I grow the more I am confirmed in what I have done—in my earliest faith—the more I am confirmed in my optimism, my democracy.

May 18, 1888

America is not all in all—the sum total: she is only to contribute her contribution to the big scheme. . . . let it

be something worth while—something exceptional, en-
nobling.

May 7, 1888

America . . . has accomplished the greatest results in
all things except literature—in all features of modern life
except literature, which is the greatest, noblest, divinest, of
all: and there she is simply an absorber, an automatic
listener, with no eye, ear, arm, heart, her own. If it was
necessary—I hope to God it will never be necessary—she
would excel all other races, states, in military glory, also,
sorry as that is, sorry—O sorry—as it is.

July 7, 1888

There's nothing I should like better than to write six or a
dozen lines . . . giving in a few words, the picture of the
revolution days—the glooms, despairs, sufferings, horrors,
suspicions, of that time: the sprinkly trailing of faith through
it all, the final victory. Then show how vastly, vastly greater
that is than the celebration of it we have been having this
past week: the dull speeches, platitudes . . .

May 4, 1889

I believe in the higher patriotism—not, my country
whether or no, God bless it and damn the rest!—no, not
that—but my country, to be kept big, to grow bigger, to
lead the procession, not in conquest, however, but in inspira-
tion.

August 5, 1888

All the real problems, the fundamentals, are yet ahead of
us—will have to be tackled by us or by our children or

theirs . . . life and death challenges which will line us up fiercely on this side or that.

November 10, 1888

. . . I feel myself that the American is being made but is not made: much of him is yet in the state of dough: the loaf is not yet given shape. He will come—our American.

May 24, 1888

· ·

AUTOGRAPH HUNTERS

· ·

W. brighter physically than yesterday, yet "still strangely languid." "It is getting to be difficult for me even to walk across the room." Very cheerful. Almost merry here and there in the talk. "My today's mail has been chiefly an autograph mail. . . . Not a day but the autograph hunter is on my trail—chases me, dogs me! sometimes two or three appear in the very same mail. Their subterfuges, deceptions, hypocrisies, are curious, nasty, yes damnable. I will get a letter from a young child—a young reader—this is her first book—she has got fond of me—she should be encouraged in her fine ambitions—would I not &c &c—and I would *not*, of course—why should I? I can see the grin of an old deceiver in such letters."

August 3, 1888

· · · · · · · · · · · · · · ·

. . . oh these autographites! they are from everlasting to everlasting!

April 2, 1889

I have no rigid rules with regard to autographs: I mainly refuse them . . .

April 6, 1889

....

THE BODY

....

7.45 P.M. W. reading the Bible. The daylight was near gone. He huddled up against it. . . .

W. entered into frank talk touching his health. I had asked my usual questions. He responded: "I have felt very well to-day: have had no visitors: best of all got a splendid —oh! a splendid!—effective bath: the best, the completest, since I was thrown on my back here. I got to-day what I call my currying, too—rubbing: I have a brush for it. I at first intended to have Ed bring the big tub into the room and fill it with water so I could take my bath right here: but I got to the bathroom—Ed helped me—and so got my swab in the old way. Ed is very stalwart—handled me well—helped me with the currying." He takes to Ed. Calls him "brawny—a powerful ally." . . . "Rubbing is good for everybody but is especially valuable to me—stands me in place of exercise: I need something, oh! so badly—something that will stir

me up like the sun and the air, of which I am now deprived:
I am a prisoner here, almost denied the light of day."

November 8, 1888

....

I can write, read, work: I find I can laugh, cry, be myself,
still, in most ways: I suppose I shouldn't kick because I
can't climb mountains.

February 10, 1889

Only when imprisoned is this way, as I have been for
close to a year now, can anyone realize what happiness
resides in the feet and knees—how much depends upon your
locomotive powers.

April 6, 1889

In fibre, muscle, organically: in build, arm, leg, chest,
belly—in physical equipment—I started superbly—no one
more so—more gifted, blessed.

November 30, 1888

It is wonderful, when you come to think of it, how much
of a man is centred in his belly: the belly is the radiant force
distributing life.

June 15, 1888

. . . there's some sort of intimate association between a
man's belly and his soul that no amount of spirituality can
get rid of.

January 31, 1889

I have belly aches and head aches and leg aches and all other kinds of damned aches but I hain't got no acheless insomnia: thank God for that!

September 21, 1888

. . . I am now passing through a bad period. Digestion is poor—poor indeed—I am in a bad way: belly, bladder, catarrh—my brain, physical brain—all are in discomfortableation.

August 19, 1889

Considering the condition of the rest of my body the immunity enjoyed by my topknot is marvellous—even surprises me.

February 12, 1889

I never get nervous: I have heard about it in others: it never affects me. I remember, my friends always remarked it, that in crises, I never was disturbed or gave out any consciousness of danger—as, indeed, I did not feel it. It has always been so: it is a part of my ancestral quality persisting and saving.

June 2, 1889

It is remarkable how men will stay and stay. Such men must have a wonderful background somewhere—some grand physical base—some sane bottom, eternal, we could say, in its purity of composition.

April 28, 1889

. . . the body is stubborn: it craves bodily presences: it has its own peculiar tenacities—we might say aspirations as well as desires.

February 10, 1889

It's as if I said I don't like the way God made my thumb: I think thumbs should be different: besides, thumbs and forefingers would be better off if they changed places: presto! I'll do what God neglected to do. That's no sort of sense at all. We must have the cares, the diseases, the dyspepticisms, all expressed along with the joy, the health, the wholesome inertia, that round out every representative personality.

February 7, 1889

By nature, by observation, by the doctors, I have learned that the thing to do when I am down is to rely upon the *vis,* as it is called—the inherited forces: to lay low—attempt nothing—rest—recuperate: if the *vis* comes to the rescue— meets the peril—well and good: then for another lease! But if it does not, then all may as well be given up at once.

December 25, 1888

. . . he was always a wise man with his body—never squandered it.

July 13, 1889

After all, there's nothing makes up for the body: when the body gives out a man's about ready to pass in his checks:

whatever's to happen hereafter, a man minus a body is of no use here. That's why the art preservative of all the arts of living is the conservation of the body.

February 11, 1889

....

BOOKS

....

6.30 P.M. W. lying on bed. Ed entered with me lighting gas. Ed said that W. "spent a day in much the same condition as last night." W. admitted that he was better: "but I am still weak—still far gone." Had eaten, however, and was manifestly stronger. Voice, manner, willingness to talk —all testified to it. He stayed on the bed for some time after I arrived, talking binder and all that. Couldn't get stitched sample to-day. Oldach rather testy about it. W. disappointed but calm. Oldach spoke of the stitching of books —the style of two centuries ago—"the old-time style"—and that of the present. "But nobody wants the old style now." W. said: "Let us be the exception: let us be the odd fellow: let us get the old stitch." Then added: "Binding illustrates all life. Show a man a house—one that may be plain but in and out everything that is honest, durable: he shakes his head: is there not something more? So you show him a reverse case—show, ornament, external bother: he at once applauds!"

November 30, 1888

....

. . . I sometimes find myself more interested in book making than in book writing: the way books are made—that always excites my curiosity: the way books are written— that only attracts me once in a great while.

February 27, 1889

I want no autocrat editions.

August 17, 1888

All my own tastes are towards books you can easily handle —put into your pocket.

July 13, 1888

I have long teased my brain with visions of a handsome little book at last . . . for the pocket. That would tend to induce people to take me along with them and read me in the open air: I am nearly always successful with the reader in the open air.

August 21, 1888

I like chapters in books to end short of a page—it pleases my eye better so.

June 19, 1888

My idea of a book page is an open one . . . words broadly spaced, lines with a grin, page free altogether: none huddled. Some printed pages seem to have a hump in the back.

June 5, 1888

Books are like men—the best of them have flaws. Thank God for the flaws!

May 18, 1888

Let's be honest with each other, even if the book is a bigwig. If we think a book's damned tiresome let's say it's damned tiresome and not say "how do you do?—come again."

July 19, 1888

. . . books have their own way of disappearing without being visibly despatched.

February 15, 1889

The best man in the world is the man who has absorbed books—great books—made the most of them—yet remains unspoiled—remains a man. It is marvellous what capacity books have for destroying as well as making a man.

June 6, 1888

CENSORSHIP

When I got there W. was fast asleep. I stayed in Ed's room till I heard W. stirring—probably half an hour. Then I passed in and had a short talk with him. Light down, room all closed, perceptible odor of burning wood. W. sitting on the edge of the bed for a few minutes, then lying down again. Had this been a better day? "I don't know: I think rather not: only mostly like other days." . . .

Proposed to take a bath to-day but when the time came his zest had flown. Read Press and Record this forenoon: also the local papers—Post, Courier. . . . We talked of the Rossetti letters. W. wished it. . . . Was very vehement about the expurgations. "Of course I see now as clearly as I did then how big and fine Rossetti was about it all. . . . But I now feel somehow as if none of the changes should have been made. . . . I doubt if I would do the thing over again that way. Rossetti himself used his margin with great tact . . . was miraculously circumspect. But an expurgation means a lot more always than it looks as if it meant—has far-reaching consequences: like one move on the chessboard that moves so much else with it—imposes other moves: so we must look out—must not compromise unless it's a life and death issue."

December 17, 1888

....

. . . I have heard nothing but expurgate, expurgate, expurgate, from the day I started. Everybody wants to expurgate something—this, that, the other thing. If I accepted all the suggestions there wouldn't be one leaf of the Leaves left. . . . Expurgation is apology—yes, surrender —yes, an admission that something or other was wrong. . . . Expurgate, expurgate—apologize, apologize: get down on your knees. . . . I must expurgate, expurgate, pick up my skirts and run back to nature: beg nature's pardon and be good hereafter.

May 14, 1888

Damn the expurgated books! I say damn 'em! The dirtiest book in all the world is the expurgated book.

May 9, 1888

I want the utmost freedom—even the utmost license— rather than any censorship: censorship is always ignorant, always bad: whether the censor is a man of virtue or a hypocrite seems to make no difference: the evil is always evil. Under any responsible social order decency will always take care of itself.

May 18, 1888

. . . I would never permit the text to be tampered with —not for any edition, not for ten thousand editions: it's a mistake: it's like going back . . .

December 17, 1888

. . . I hate all censorships, big and little: I'd rather have everything rotten than everything hypocritical or puritani-cal, if that was the alternative, as it is not. I'd dismiss all monitors, guardians, without any ceremony whatsoever.

February 21, 1889

Anyway you look at it, I'm not a bloomin' success from the market point of view. I find that with regard to the abridged books I hate 'em more and more. I hate the idea of being put somewhere with the harm taken out of me, as good house-wives alter Tomcats to make them respectable in the neighborhood.

October 2, 1888

Whitman during the Civil War. Charles E. Feinberg Collection

CHURCH & CLERGY

W. said: "I have often tried to put myself in the place of a minister—to imagine the forty and odd corns he must avoid treading on." Laughingly: "I often get mad at the ministers—they are almost the only people I do get mad at —yet they, too, have their reasons for being. If a man will once consent to be a minister he must expect ruin."

May 12, 1888

. . . the ministers are practically done for, the stars in their courses are against them: however they struggle, whatever front they maintain, the universe is against their impossible explications: their methods have passed out for good.

February 4, 1889

The world is through with sermonizing—with the necessity for it: the distinctly preacher ages are nearly gone. I am not sorry.

May 5, 1888

I am not willing to admit that we have any further serious use for the old style authoritative preacher. . . . we might as well think of curing people of the measles, the smallpox, what not, by mere sermonizings, yawpings, as of saving their souls by such tactics. . . . I do not mean by this that the mind may not be an aid in the cure of disease, in the saving of souls, as they call it—yes—I only mean that no amount of formal, salaried, petitioning of God will serve to work out the result aimed for.

May 6, 1888

. . . all preaching is a weariness to me. . . . We have the stock phrases in books—the stock canvases in art: well, so we have the stock stupidities in sermons. . . . I am always impatient of the churches—they are not God's own— they rather fly in the face of the real providences.

May 20, 1888

. . . the Bible in the hands of the preachers: nearly anything can be proved from it: there's no assumption so preposterous but that it can be bolstered by some text, some chapter, from somewhere in the book. When the verbalism does not seem to fit they force it without scruple this way or that till it looks to be right in shape and size.

February 4, 1889

To any man who thinks—to any man alive to the revelations of modern science—it is an insult to offer the doctrines of the church: it is as if you approached him to say: "What a damned fool you are, anyway!"

May 20, 1888

Their [the clergy's] teaching is mostly impudence—their knowledge is mostly ignorance—they are arrogant, spoiled.

May 12, 1888

What in hell's name is a minister's point of view. He does not approach life as a man or as an American or as a lover or even a hater but from a minister's point of view.

May 4, 1888

The damnable psalming, praying, deaconizing of our day is made too much the liberal cover for all sorts of sins, iniquities.

April 13, 1889

The ministry is spoiled with arrogance: it takes all sorts of vagaries, impudences, invasions, for granted: it even seizes the key to the bedroom and the closet.

May 1, 1888

Ministers are rarely friendly to me—perhaps are a little more tolerant than they were at the start, though damned little. There have been some exceptions—a few orthodox preachers who were far more revolutionary than they supposed themselves to be.

May 11, 1888

I have met many preachers in my time—some of the sleek kind, but many of them personally good fellows, who treated me well. Always remember, though I hate preaching I do not hate preachers.

July 28, 1888

The instant a priest becomes a man I am on his side—I no longer oppose him.

May 12, 1888

Men make churches: men may destroy churches. I see no use for the church: it lags superfluous on the stage.

May 6, 1888

The whole ideal of the church is low, loathsome, horrible —a sort of moral negation—as if men got down in the mud to worship—delighting in the filth: out of touch entirely with the great struggles of contemporary humanity.

May 6, 1888

To me the negative virtues of the church are the most menacing, to me the most abhorrent, of all the professed virtues.

May 3, 1888

I never made any vows to go or not to go: I went, at intervals, but anywhere—to no one place: was a wanderer: went oftenest in my earlier life—gradually dropped off altogether: today a church is a sort of offense to me. I never had any "views"—was always free—made no pledges, adopted no creeds, never joined parties or "bodies."

July 28, 1888

The church is no place for a man after he has got his growth.

August 23, 1888

I think one of the churches as good as the other: that may seem extreme, but it is my impression: as good and as bad as the other: as safe and as perilous as the other: as institutions they are both menacing, to be guarded against.

November 8, 1888

We seem to require all kinds of bigots to complete the chapter of our sorrows—Methodist bigots, Presbyterian bigots, the bigots for the Bible, the bigots against the Bible, Quaker bigots stiffer than their hats: all sorts, all sorts: we need them all to finish off the ornament of our hari-kari world.

August 5, 1888

. . . I like the sects—I feel of them as a doctor (does) of pimples on the face—it is better for them to come out than to be hidden underneath the exterior—a hundred per-cent better. Pimples are a thing we can fight, but insidious hidden processes defy battle.

September 14, 1889

CONDUCT

8 P.M. W. reading Boston Transcript. "A monotonous paper," he said, "but on a rather high level: monotonously good, we might say." I had with me the six hundred and more first folds of the big book. As he saw my big bundle he asked: "What have you got there—what is all that?" I

replying: "Some work for you to do." "Ah! the sheets! Hurrah!" Then he stopped himself: "I'd better wait until I get them all signed before I yell hurrah!" Fixed the sheets carefully on the floor within reach. Contemplated them with pleasure. "This looks like getting something done: I'll be getting quite proud of myself by and bye—or of you, rather, for you are the one who is oiling the machine and keeping the fires up these days.". . .

When I said: "McKay thinks November Boughs will sell," W. replied: "Let him go on believing there's no hell! . . . I'd venture to say that nine out of every ten people who happened into a book store would take a fling at anything they saw there that was novel or new. The casual observer is always a critic first—and but rarely a good one, either."

October 8, 1888

....

It is often said: better to have this ire out than in. I am not so sure about that: I question whether a fellow has any excuse for hitting out right and left fore and aft on the slightest provocation. While it might do him good to hit what about the man he hits?

October 11, 1888

That is a very prevalent fashion, especially in America, when a fellow gets completely stumped, he takes refuge in that—"It is a difference of opinion!"

July 14, 1889

A man who proposes something new and will not give people time to see it is not worthy of his message.

June 17, 1888

It does a man good to turn himself inside out once in a while: to sort of turn the tables on himself: to look at himself through other eyes—especially skeptical eyes, if he can. It takes a good deal of resolution to do it: yet it should be done—no one is safe until he can give himself such a drubbing: until he can shock himself out of his complacency. Think how we go on believing in ourselves—which in the main is all right (what could we ever do if we didn't believe in ourselves?): but if we don't look out we develop a bumptious bigotry—a colossal self-satisfaction, which is worse for a man than being a damned scoundrel.

December 18, 1888

. . . there are so many dangers—so many ways for the innocent to be betrayed: in the clutter, clatter, crack of metropolitan ambitions, jealousies, bribes, so many ways for a man, unless he is a giant, unless he is possessed of brutal strength and independence—so many ways for him to go to the devil.

January 1, 1889

It is a good and safe rule, always to take care to be introduced to the fellow you don't want to meet. These do us the most good. It is not a man's friends from whom he gets the most benefit—of course you know that as well as I do—but often the man who despises you, won't have you on any terms, is most rich in benefits.

April 29, 1889

I always remember that sometimes a fellow has to choose to do the unpleasant thing. "Doing your duty" the preachers and the mothers call it. Sometimes I do my duty: not always : not because I live by any special method. Duty, duty. It is a free word—it is a slave word. The mothers make it a free word—the preachers make it a slave word.

April 26, 1888

It's a profound problem : teaching morals : they should be taught—yet also not taught : sometimes I say one shouldn't teach morals to anybody : when I see the harm that morals do I almost hate seeing people good : then there's another side to it : then I see how necessary it is that we should have a code, live with it, die for it.

January 27, 1889

My old daddy used to say it's some comfort to a man if he must be an ass anyhow to be his own kind of an ass.

July 26, 1888

....

CRITICS

....

The cooler day has had a brightening effect upon W. He regains no strength, but feels less depressed physically. He deplored his weakness, though quite satisfied to have things as well as they are. He makes no motion, however, towards going down stairs. Read and wrote more considerably than usual today. . . . He sat much of the day across the room from the bed working in a mild way. His raw product is about him, on the table, the floor, in boxes and baskets, on chairs, and pretty nearly all things he may need are within reaching distance. At his foot is the pitcher of ordinary (never iced) water, which he takes up from time to time and draws from copiously. Books are piled promiscuously about, his will remains on the box-corner where he placed it when it was drawn up—letters, envelopes, are scattered over the floor,—autographed volumes hang on the edges of the table-leaves, chairs, the sofa—everything seeming in disorder. My impression of W's appearance . . . : His face is not as full as it was: he has nervous irritations: there are lines, down-lines, never until now in his cheeks. . . . W's room is a large one, considering the house—it has three north windows—one door opening from it into the hallway, another into a connecting apartment. In this latter (he never works here) are most of his stored papers, books, and with them the Morse heads [plaster busts of Walt Whitman made by Sidney H. Morse]—three or four of them—and boxes more or less laden with letters, &c. Often he points me about the rooms: "Poor as these are, they are a comfort to me—my own—giving me freedom: such freedom as I am competent yet to enjoy.". . .

He spoke of George Ripley as a man superlatively equipped for the office of critic. . . . "There are critics and critics. You don't know the tribe as I do—the damned mean stuff they are often made of—the very poison (not the salt) of the earth. Some of my opponents are fairly on the other side—belong there, are honest, I respect them: others are malignants—are of the snake order."

August 9, 1888

....

. . . a critic. Do you know a more dangerous business? A critic writes about a book—says yes to it, or no: blesses it, curses it. How does he come to his result? When he takes up a book he is himself uncertain—what he finally decides to say about it depends upon his mood—perhaps upon the condition of his stomach, the liver.

May 29, 1888

The great function of the critic is to say bright things— sparkle, effervesce: probably three-quarters, perhaps even more, of them do not take the trouble to examine what they start out to criticize—to judge a man from his own standpoint, to even find out what that standpoint is.

January 28, 1889

Most of these book reviews so-called are echoes of echoes: the fellows don't seem to have a bit of originality: they run after each other like sheep: one says a thing: then the other says a thing: then they chorus together—the whole kit and crew: they say, one, two, three, damn so and so: they say four, five, six, save so and so: that's the way they proceed: like so many monkeys on the limb of a tree chattering in concert.

December 30, 1888

Every whipper-snapper of a reviewer, instead of trying to get at the motive of a book or an incident, sets out sharply to abuse a fellow because he don't accomplish what he never aimed for and sometimes would not have if he could.

September 15, 1888

I am not thin-skinned about opposition: it is being misunderstood—that's what tantalizes me.

July 17, 1888

Whitman about 50. Photograph by Frank Pearsall

What I object to are the sneakers—the men who hit from the rear. Criticism is a matter of course—often the best food: the right negative word spoken at the right time saves many a soul. Criticism is a necessary test—the passage of fire: we have got to meet it—there is no escape.

July 16, 1888

I don't mind the simple, straight-out negative—indeed, I like it: I don't mind the fellows who say without a tremor: "Here, damn you, Walt Whitman, what do you mean by all this nonsense. To hell with you, Walt Whitman: to hell with you! to hell with you!" That don't sound bad—on the contrary it sounds very good—it is tonic. But when a fellow comes along, convinced and not convinced, hungry for your society and afraid of your society, blowing hot and cold, with praise on his lips that had better be blame, you are at your wit's end to know how to meet him.

August 2, 1888

If you have not experienced a direct encounter with the monitors, critics, censors, you can have no idea of the venoms, jealousies, meannesses, spites, which chiefly characterize their opposition. It has been a rallying cry with a little group of men in the country: down Walt Whitman—down him in any way, by any method, with any weapon you can—but down him—drive him into obscurity, hurry him into oblivion! But suppose Walt Whitman stays, stays, is stubborn, stays again, stays again, will not be downed?

August 9, 1888

The critics are always after the style: style, style, style, damn it style, till your stomach is turned: everything must go for style. Nearly everybody who takes up Leaves of

Grass stops with the style, as if that was all there is to it. Nearly everybody—every fellow almost without exception —founders on that rock—goes down hopelessly—a victim of rules, canons, cultures.

July 10, 1888

When you talk to me of "style" it is as though you had brought me artificial flowers . . . I used to stop at Eighth street there, near Market, and look at the artificial flowers made with what marvellous skill. But then I would say: What's the use of the wax flowers when you can go out for yourself and pick the real flowers? That's what I think when people talk to me of "style," "style," as if style alone and of itself was anything. . . . the style is to have no style.

May 5, 1888

. . . better to have people stirred against you if they can't be stirred for you—better that than not to stir them at all. I think I first thrived on opposition: the allies came later.

May 30, 1888

I have asked myself in the face of criticism of my own work: "Should I reply—should I expose, denounce, explain?" But my final conviction has always been that there is no better reply than silence. Besides, I am conscious that I have peculiarly laid myself open to ridicule—to the shafts of critics, readers, glittering paragraphers: yet I am profoundly sure of one thing: that never, never, has even calumny deflected me from the course I had determined to pursue.

January 28, 1889

Sometimes I get the impulse to run away—to get beyond all the seeing and hearing of criticism: to just write, to perhaps publish, but to refuse to have anything further to do with what happens or does not happen.

February 22, 1889

Every time I criticise a man or a book I feel as if I had done something wrong. The criticism may be justified in letter and spirit—yet I feel guilty—feel like a man who ought to go to jail. . . . I hate to think any man may not write the best books—any man. When I find any man don't I am disappointed and say things. How lucky is the man who don't say things!

April 25, 1888

Why should I take judgment in hand? I throw away all my weapons—all, all: all weapons of harm—every weapon: I want to meet every man, worst man or best man, with the open hand.

May 12, 1888

CULTURE

I asked W.: "What would you say of the University and Modern Life?" "I wouldn't say anything: I'd rather be excused." "But suppose you couldn't dodge it—had to say something?" He took my quizzing genially this time. "You know: I have said everything to you before. I have nothing new to announce." "But suppose you had to talk?" "Had to? I never have to: but you know my feeling about the colleges: I do not object to anything they do that will enrich the popular life—emphasize the forces of democracy: the trouble is that so much they do is bent the other way—seems to me simply hopeless scholartism or encourages reaction: is bookishness rather than revelation: is not vital, brutal, instant instinct but the distillation of distillations God knows how many removes from origins." I said: "Well—I got you to say something, anyhow!" He added: "Yes, you did: I don't take it back: so much of the work we might be warranted in expecting the university to do has to be done outside universities today: the university is only contemporary at the best: it is never prophetic: it goes, but not in advance: often, indeed . . . has its eyes set in the back of its head." I asked: "Isn't this all inevitable as long as the university is an aristocratic rather than a democratic institution?" W.: "I do not deny it . . .". Then he broke into a laugh: "Those university folk, you can see, wouldn't care a tinker's damn to have me address them on the subject: at the same time I believe every man should have his fling: so let them go on talking their savior-of-society nonsense: let them go on believing there's no hell: there's a day of reckoning ahead." I interrupted: "Then what will happen?" "Then we'll have more schools or no schools: schools from bottom to top, for all or for none."

March 19, 1889

....

College men as a rule would rather get along without me: they go so far, the best of them—then stop: some of them don't go at all.

June 8, 1888

. . . I need toning down or up or something to get me in presentable form for the ceremonials of seats of learning. You must understand that I never blame anybody or any organization or any university for discovering my cloven hoof. I am like the diplomists who are *non grata*: I can't be tolerated by the kings, lords, lackeys, of culture: in the verbal courts of the mighty. I am mostly outlawed —and no wonder.

January 29, 1889

. . . the best college-bred man gets to some extent the taint of bookishness, artificiality.

February 27, 1889

It's all one: the lords and ladies of culture: they're as abhorrent to me as the lords and ladies of titles.

April 5, 1889

What I object to in so much that we call education, culture, scholarship, is that it seems to invest its avatars with contempt for the elemental qualities in character.

May 30, 1888

We talk about salvation: we need most of all to be saved from ourselves: our own hells, hates, jealousies, thieveries: we need most to be saved from our own priests—the priests of the churches, the priests of the arts: we need that salvation the worst way.

January 9, 1889

DEATH

8 P.M. W. reading the Mrs. Carlyle letters. Held the book sort of in the air as he read. Eyes wide open. Hat on. Entire attitude one of great interest. Light burned brightly. Saw me—laid the book down: "Howdy? Howdy?" extending his right hand. They had cleared the room up a bit today. Complains some of his eyes. Fire burns in his room. Very hot but calls the room "just about comfortable." Likes to keep the stove door open—to feed the fire from time to time. Still hates to be helped. "I'd rather die helping myself than live being helped."

October 9, 1888

. . . I am cheerful today. The fact that I am consciously staring death in the face don't make me less cheerful: even death has its advantages—and death has its to-morrow.

September 20, 1888

There's the book—the dear book—forever waiting—and I seem to be more feeble than ever. But there's no use dying now when there's still a job of work to do.

July 2, 1888

Some night it will be a last kiss—a last good-night—but I hope not just yet—not till the books are done.

May 19, 1888

After all I do not kick—I am willing to take what comes —death or life—half life, half death—everything. I clearly perceive that I shall never get back where I was—I have slipped down a notch or two. But I don't care. My only concern is for the work—the book. I don't want to sink— drown—before the book is out. . . . I have made up my mind not to worry—not to let even the worst upset me— not to look with dread upon anything. . . . we must not be afraid of the worst—indeed, we must invite the worst— must bear all, brave all, and, coming to the test, throw or be thrown by it. The question has come back to me in fifty different forms as I lie here footing up my accounts with the Almighty!

July 5, 1888

. . . in a sense I am in a hurry—one day to all of us— to all of us—there comes the closing of the doors—the entrances—the exits—so that one may pass no more out or in —so that if there's something to do, it is well for a fellow to do it—to do it without pause.

August 14, 1889

When a man gets old he has confirmed habits—has ways of his own which the winds blowing however hard or righteously could not displace: they are his to last out his life. They all give me good advice which I can't follow. I . . . must be left to die in my own way.

September 26, 1888

. . . your dog here is too old to learn any new tricks: to stop at the door of the tomb and study a new a b c .

August 7, 1888

Death is like being invited out to a good dinner.
February 5, 1889

Most formal funerals are insults: they belittle the dead. If anything should be honest a funeral should be honest.
June 11, 1888

If I keep on fooling with one will and another I won't know which is my last.
June 29, 1888

DOCTORS & DRUGS

. . . several questions about which I had to confer with W. I went . . . this noon, reaching 328 at a quarter past twelve. Found Harned there with two of his children, Mrs. Davis also, all of them in the parlor, anxiously regarding W., who lay on the sofa. What was the matter? My alarm was instant. But W. was very cheerful: "I seem to have had since last night three strokes of a paralytic character— shocks, premonitions. That's all there is to it. Don't worry about it, boy." He held my hand warmly and firmly. When he drove off from Harned's yesterday with Doctor Bucke he was in great good humor and (for him) apparent health. In the evening he undertook to sponge himself, in his own room, alone, and while so engaged fell to the floor, finding himself unable to move or to call for assistance, lying there, he thought, helplessly, for several hours. . . . This morning two perhaps lighter attacks had followed. . . . Harned was present when this occurred. No doctor there. "Don't get a doctor," commanded W., adding humorously: "I think of it this way, you know: that if the doctors come I shall not only have to fight the disease but fight them, whereas if I am left alone I have but the one foe to contend with."

June 4, 1888

....

I have no great faith in or fear of doctors—they don't seem to do much good or much harm.

July 9, 1888

I don't think any of the doctors—the best doctors— have arrived at my doctrine yet—that each person who comes to be treated, has to be treated as a person, not as a member of a class.

July 18, 1889

. . . a specialist much as we know doctors to be nowa- days—as it is said doctors must be—not doctors of the whole man, of the body however affected—but controlling a department only—ear, eye, teeth, brain, what-not—doing that well—oh! grandly superlatively well, to be sure—but only departmentarily after all.

April 29, 1889

There seemed to be in him [a soldier in an army hospi- tal] as in all of us at some hours that suspicion—what do the doctors know?—what a mass of solid pretense after all! what the devil is the use of diets, abstentions, prohibi- tions, squeamishnesses?

December 6, 1888

Ah! these doctors! . . . do they know much? . . . I love doctors and hate their medicine.

July 8, 1888

I find that the drugs always excessively affect me—almost violently—that my nature seems set against them. It is true, that the drugs may affect the end for which they are applied, but I find they effect more, too—so much more, that the balance of good is on the wrong side—that I come out minus.

July 18, 1889

The trouble is not with the doctors alone, but the patients : the patients, too, are responsible for the tomfoolery. The patient wants the worth of his money, so he must have a powder or two—some medicine—what not. Then the whole medicine business is a sort of a now you see it now you don't affair, sifted down, don't you think?

January 15, 1889

. . . it's all got to go—the drug theory: there's something wrong about it: it's a poisonous viperous notion: it does not seem to fit with what we know of the human body —with the physical something or other and the mental something or other going together : they doctor a man as a disease not as a man : a part of him—doctor a part of him : a leg, a belly, an eye : they ignore the rest : as if it wasn't true that the seat of the trouble in most cases is not at the point of demonstration but way below somewhere : oh! I am impatient about it : it riles me—makes me say ugly things.

December 14, 1888

It is one of the admonitions of my Doctor not to see people—not to talk: but then I am a disobedient subject: I only regard professional advice so far—not farther: I decide limits for myself after all.

February 12, 1889

. . . improved? I don't know. The Doctor talks—I accept his talk—but that don't conclude the matter. The shoemaker tells his customer that the shoe just fits but the customer feels the pinch: the fellow who wears the shoe always knows most about the pinch.

October 3, 1888

From the medical point of view they tell me I'm getting on all right, but from the point of view of my own comfort I'm in a pretty boggy condition indeed. But so the doctor feels all right about it I don't suppose it matters what I feel. I like to see the doctors comfortable, anyway.

June 30, 1888

DRESS

To W.'s in the forenoon. "I'm going up to Tom's for tea—you will be there?" He was trying on a new red tie. "Red has life in it—our men mostly look like funerals, undertakers: they set about to dress as gloomy as they can."

April 15, 1888

It seems to me that two things are indispensable in tailoring—to give a man the best buttons and provide him with plenty and strong and big pockets. I always lay this down as the law to anyone who works for me.

May 30, 1889

The next thing to being fashionable is to be unfashionable.

July 30, 1888

One belongs with the other, high hat and church—each equally detestable.

May 19, 1889

EDITORS

W. sometimes has what he calls "house-cleaning days." He puts aside some waste for me on these occasions. I always take along what he gives me. I know what will be its ultimate value as biographical material. He rarely or never takes that into account. For instance today he said: "I would burn such stuff up—or tear it up—anything to get it out of the road." He laughed in handing me three letters done up in a string. "They are all declinations of poems," he remarked: "from different men at different times." Then after a pause: "These editorial dictators have a right to dictate: they know what their magazines are made for. I notice that we all get cranky about them when they say 'No, thank you,' but after all somebody has got to decide: I am sure I never have felt sore about any negative experience I have had, and I have had plenty of it—yes, more that than the other—mostly that, in fact."

April 12, 1888

....

There is no appeal from the editor: he is a necessary autocrat.

May 19, 1888

I sometimes growl a little about the editors but after all they are a good lot—they do the best they can. Besides, I am an incongruity to most of them—I make the sort of noise they don't like—I upset some things they do like: why should I expect to be received? The wonder is not that I am sometimes kicked out—the wonder is that anybody will receive me. I used to worry over it, just a little—resent it, too, just a little: I am past that now.

May 27, 1888

Who has had more experience of the nether kind than I have? I think everything that could happen to a rejected author has happened one time or another to me.

May 20, 1888

I do not feel sore when I am refused, but I hate to be pitched out head first without a chance to open the door for myself and go out.

August 28, 1888

Photograph of Whitman by Frank Pearsall

....

FAME

....

Took to Ferguson today (after meeting and receiving the package from Mrs. Davis at the ferry) the copy for Sands at Seventy [a group of poems]. . . . Then in with W. this evening to confer. Much discussion . . . W. tremendously pleased with the proofsheets. "They are the best I have ever received—those fellows must be first-class: I have written a note to say so—enclosed it in the package." In this note W. extended his thanks to the foreman, proofreader and compositors of the Ferguson office. . . . wants now "to go straight ahead with the book," adding: "I am almost in a hurry, which is remarkable for me. And besides, I have quite a feeling for the printers—for the two you said were laid off: I do not want them to suffer on my account: Ferguson got them for me—I should keep them going." . . .

General Sheridan is very sick. W. spoke of it. "I think it comes a great deal from high living. These military men have a curious experience—first on the field, inured to all possible hardship: there they do their work—get their fame. Then peace comes—then they are coddled, fêted, dined, out of sense—out of health: in fact, ruined."

June 1, 1888

....

Old men who have enjoyed a certain amount of fame—done great work—require to be fêted, noticed, flattered, commended, cultivated by the ladies, taken the rounds of clubs, of the towns, of meals—of dinners and suppers. I don't seem to like that sort of attention myself.

May 28, 1888

It is a new experience to be successful: I always seem to know what to do with failure but success is a puzzle to me.

May 9, 1888

. . . as the fellow did who unexpectedly found himself in heaven. He didn't ask himself whether he deserved it—he just kept quiet and stayed.

July 4, 1888

When a man gets in the collections—then he thinks himself secure: it is like going to church: the fellows are in their places regularly, hear the sermon, pray, sing, go home again, think the whole thing done, though it is by no means done—is not even commenced.

March 4, 1889

FAMILY

W. said: "My brother Jeff, from St. Louis—civil engineer there: until nine months ago for some time in the Water Department—has been here today." Remarked in this connection: "No one of my people—the people near to me—ever had any time for Leaves of Grass—thought it more than an ordinary piece of work, if that." Not even his mother? "No—I think not—even her: there is, as I say, no one in my immediate family who follows me out on that line. My dear mother had every general faith in me; that is where she stopped. She stood before Leaves of Grass mystified, defeated."

May 29, 1888

•••••••••••••••••

The reality, the simplicity, the transparency, of my dear, dear mother's life, was responsible for the main things in the letters as in Leaves of Grass itself. How much I owe her! It could not be put in a scale—weighed: it could not be measured—be even put in the best words: it can only be apprehended through the intuitions. Leaves of Grass is the flower of her temperament active in me.

August 9, 1888

It is lucky for me if I take after the women of my ancestry, as I hope I do: they were so superior, so truly the more pregnant forces in our family history.

April 28, 1888

I started well—am built up bodily on a good base: I had a good father and mother, just as my father and mother again had good fathers and mothers.

April 6, 1889

I used to be Walter—started that way: then I became Walt. My father was Walter. He had a right to Walter. I had to be distinguished from him so I was made Walt. My friends kicked: Walter looked and sounded better: and so forth, and so forth. But Walt stuck.

May 8, 1888

. . . I am of the clan: the Whitman clan—the blood: it appeals to me . . . I am wholly loyal, even sort of tribal . . .

January 15, 1889

It is the Whitman trait to love women, babies, and cattle . . .

June 16, 1889

Being a blood brother to a man don't make him a real brother in the final sense of that term.

January 15, 1889

A man's family is the people who love him—the people who comprehend him.

January 13, 1889

HANDWRITING

W. up in his room moving about and closing the blinds when I arrived, 8 P.M. "Day not a bad one for me," he said at once. . . . Had written nothing—"not even letters to Bucke, Burroughs and Kennedy—to whom I owe my biggest debts. . . . I had a card from Kennedy today,—a scrambly hasty upset characteristic postal. Did you ever notice that Kennedy's writing sort of stands on its head?"

July 10, 1888

•••••••••••••••••

Why in heaven's name a man will write a hell of a hand —good people, too, often the best people (especially the English: they are the worst offenders)—I can't say: an insufferable affectation, negligence, carelessness.

February 8, 1889

. . . I still say to the army of the illegibles, for God's sake do the best you can to write so we can at least get some clues to what you are trying to say.

March 8, 1889

My writing has been clear from the start—almost from boyhood: not beautiful, but legible.

July 21, 1888

. . . I like the mammoth pens: they are easy to write with. . . . I am sensitive—I especially hate the little bits of pens—the dwarf ladylike pens: I don't seem to be able to do anything fullsized with them: they interfere with my ideas—break my spirit.

January 30, 1889

....

HIMSELF

....

W. was joyous over what he called "a piece of the best news." What was the best news? "The Whitman Club in Boston has petered out. It failed because I sat down on it. I wrote . . . discouraging the idea. . . . I never wish to be studied in that way. I seem to need to be studied by each man for himself, not by a club. Anyway, I was agin it."

April 24, 1888

....

People often speak of me as if I was very new—original. I am in fact very old as well as very new. I don't so much come announcing new things as resuming the correct perspective on old things. I am very homely, plain, easy to know, if you take me right. Three or four years ago I spoke to some soldier boys in Brooklyn. I started by saying I did not come to reveal new things but to speak of those particular things about which all of them knew. When I see how damned hard everybody strains to say bright things, I think it well to recall them to plain facts—plain divine facts—from time to time.

May 28, 1888

I do not seem to belong to great show events—I am more like nobody than like somebody, as some funny man says—I was more used to being kicked out than asked in: I always

went to the big pow wows with the crowd, to look on, not
with the nabobs, to perform.

June 14, 1888

I must see to it, rather that I am suited than that the
public is suited. I don't know if a fellow ought to say it, but
if it might be allowed I would say: so I please myself I
don't care a damn what the public thinks of me.

August 7, 1888

I am what the boys call a stayer—I am very cautious.
. . . Thirty years ago or more a circle of *célèbres* in
phrenology gave my head a public dissection in a hall—for
one point, marked my caution very high. . . . I live even
today most conservatively. . . . I know what [Oliver Wen-
dell] Holmes said about phrenology—that you might as
easily tell how much money is in a safe feeling the knob on
the door as tell how much brain a man has by feeling the
bumps on his head: and I guess most of my friends distrust
it—but then you see I am very old fashioned—I probably
have not got by the phrenology stage yet.

June 26, 1888

I do not lack in egotism . . . the sort of egotism that is
willing to know itself as honestly as it is willing to know
third or fourth parties. Why shouldn't a man be allowed to
weigh himself? He can't do worse than go wrong: going
wrong is no hurt.

June 26, 1888

I have never praised myself where I would not if I had
been somebody else: I have merely looked myself over and

repeated candidly what I saw—the mean things and the
good things: I did so in the Leaves, I have done so in other
places: candidly faced the life in myself—my own possibilities, probabilities: reckoned up my own account, so to
speak. I know this is unusual: but is it wrong? Why should
not everybody do it?

January 4, 1889

I have made my mistakes too—have not always got
events, myself, into right perspectives: have said things that
should not have been said—have been silent when I should
have spoken: in all that, I, too, have been guilty enough.

June 17, 1888

I don't like to be thought querulous—I like to give the
biggest meanings to people, things, events, that I can.

July 2, 1888

I don't want to figure anywhere as misanthropic, sour,
doubtful: as a discourager—as a putter-out of lights.

November 3, 1888

I am more likely any time to be governed by my intuitive
than by my critical self, anyhow.

August 26, 1888

I have very little faculty or liking for books which require
charts, comparisons, references—close application—the ob-
servance of rules of logic: in the immortal words of [John]
Swinton addressed to me in a peevish humor: I have a
damned ill-regulated mind.

July 15, 1888

I am a poor hand to make promises: I never make a promise that I can avoid. I guess that's the reason I never got married; if I had set apart a day I might have begged off when the date arrived.

July 18, 1888

You know I am very arbitrary: always determined to have my own way; so much so, those who have worked for me, understood me, have adopted the method of the China-man who cut a hole to sew a patch on.

January 14, 1889

HISTORY & BIOGRAPHY

W. talked humorously of portraits, of traditions about public men. . . . "Now, there's Abraham Lincoln: people get to know his traits, his habits of life, some of his characteristics set off in the most positive relief: soon all sorts of stories are fathered on him—some of them true, some of them apocryphal—volumes of stories (stories decent and indecent) fathered on him: legitimate stories, illegitimate: and so Lincoln comes to us more or less falsified. Yet I know that the hero is after all greater than any idealization. Undoubtedly—just as the man is greater than his portrait—the landscape than the picture of it—the fact than anything we can say about the fact. While I accept the records I think we know very little of the actual. I often reflect, how very different every fellow must have been from the fellow we come upon in the myths—with the surroundings, the incidents, the push and pull of the concrete moment, all left out or wrongly set forth. It is hard to extract a man's real self—any man—from such a chaotic mass—from such historic débris."

May 6, 1888

■■■■■■■■■■■■■■■■■

. . . all along in history all sorts of stories have been fathered, mothered, on the *célèbres:* they are considered safer when you have given them some individual to nestle in.

March 1, 1889

We talk of "facts" in history. What are the facts? A good deal that gets written once is repeated and repeated, until the future comes to swear by it as gospel.

April 28, 1888

All the "great phrases" in history are no doubt fictions.

May 6, 1888

I have something of Shelley's distaste for history—so much of it is cruel, so much of it is lie. I am waiting for the historians who will tell the truth about the people—about the nobility of the people: the essential soundness of the common man. There are always—there have been always— a thousand good deeds that we say nothing about for every bad deed that we fuss over. Think of the things in everyday life—we see them everywhere—that never are exploited in print. Nobody hunts them up—nobody puts them into a story. But let one base thing happen and all the reporters of all the papers are on the spot in a minute. That don't seem to give goodness a fair deal—though I don't know: maybe goodness don't need a fair deal—maybe goodness gets along on its own account without the historian.

May 15, 1888

The masters in history have had lots of chance: they have been glorified beyond recognition: now give the other fellows a chance: glorify the average man just a bit: put in a word for his sorrows, his tragedies, just for once, just for once.

May 5, 1888

To judge of history as if all could be brought, expressed, in one fact—one little branch of knowledge—in one person! I am very impatient of stories which imply the concentration of all historical meanings in single eminent persons.

October 3, 1888

. . . it is as useless to quarrel with history as with the weather: we can prepare for the weather and prepare for history.

April 6, 1888

They used to load all their indecent stories on Lincoln: now some people are loading all their indecent interpretations on me.

August 10, 1888

. . . be sure to write about me honest: whatever you do do not prettify me: include all the hells and damns. . . . I have hated so much of the biography in literature because it is so untrue: look at our national figures how they are spoiled by liars: by the people who think they can improve on God Almighty's work—who put an extra touch on here, there, here again, there again, until the real man is no longer recognizable.

June 29, 1888

. . . the best autobiography is not built but grows.

December 21, 1888

My experience with life makes me afraid of the historian: the historian, if not a liar himself, is largely at the mercy of liars.

October 27, 1888

. . . what lying things, travesties, most all so-called histories, biographies, autobiographies, are! They make you sick—give you the bellyache! I suppose it can be said that the world still waits for its honest historian, biographer, autobiographer.

March 30, 1889

LEAVES OF GRASS

W. speaks of L. of G. as "ours." Will say, for instance, of some one or other, "he is not our friend," or "he is favorably disposed towards us," or "we must face that criticism and see what it means to us," or "that is wrong— we must brave it down." Always talks of "our portion"— ours, us, rarely says, *mine*. "This affair is our affair, not any one man's affair." Even speaks of November Boughs as "our" book. "Leaves of Grass is not one man's book but all men's book." Again: "Leaves of Grass may be only an indication—a forerunner—a crude offender against the usual canons—a barbaric road-breaker—but it still has a place, a season, I am convinced. What is that place? that season? I don't know—I give up guessing."

July 8, 1888

....

I do not look for a vast audience—for great numbers of endorsers, absorbers—just now—perhaps not even after a while. But here and there, every now and then, one, several, will raise the standard. Leaves of Grass will finally make its way. The book is like the flukes of a whale—if not graceful at least effective: never super-refined or ashamed of the animal energy that imparts power to expression.

July 16, 1888

It seems to me a man was never more fortunate than I have been in having things done just as he demands them. I never for an instant lost sight of this—lost my grip, hold, of the books: I handled them, shifted them, changed them, never yielding control of them for an instant to any one. Take the big book, for instance: whatever it is not, it certainly is what I—I alone—no other—designed it should be. Whether lost—lost at last—unaccepted, unread— whether the world listens or turns from it—there at least it is—direct from my hands, I alone being responsible for the making of it. That of itself is something high in the nature

Whitman in Brooklyn about 1870. Charles E. Feinberg Collection

of reward, if we must have reward. There is everything to tempt a man to stray—little to hold him steadfast—yet to stick must at last be its own satisfaction.

December 22, 1888

I don't say a man's old age is as important as his youth or less important than his youth: or his work—that it's as strong: that does not come in: I only say that in the larger view, in the scheme originally laid down for the Leaves, the last old age even if an old age of the dotard is as essential (if I live to old age) as the record of my first youth.

December 21, 1888

It would be ridiculous to think of Leaves of Grass belonging to any one person: at the most I am only a mouthpiece. My name occurs inside the book—that is enough if not more than enough. I like the feeling of a general partnership—as if the Leaves was anybody's who chooses just as truly as mine.

August 2, 1888

Leaves of Grass has room for everybody: if it did not make room for all it would not make room for one.

April 18, 1888

A great many years ago . . . I got into a regular row by defending the Queen—and there were Englishmen present, too. But in my philosophy—in the bottom-meanings of Leaves of Grass—there is plenty of room for all. And I, for my part, not only include anarchists, socialists, whatnot, but Queens, aristocrats.

May 26, 1889

That is what I wanted the book to be: to stand for in some sense, to testify to, the multifariousness of the universe —to include, combine, celebrate all: all: not the least jot missed: not the mouthpiece of classes, select cliques, parts, details—the choiceries of literature: no: but all, all: to utter the bad as well as the good—to participate in the common, the outcast, along with the high, the elect: to see care, oversight, everywhere: the divine working through it all: never an ending of intention: the purpose vital, evident, inveterate, to the end.

February 15, 1889

. . . I have said from the first that Leaves of Grass was not to achieve a negative recognition—was bound to be either a howling success or a stupendous failure.

August 7, 1888

More and more do I see that it is with the young man, the young woman,—that there lies the future of Leaves of Grass—that its real constituency will be these newer personalities.

August 9, 1889

I understood . . . that they originally had the Leaves in the store [Wanamaker's]—considered it—but decided finally that it would not do for them in any way to seem to back up the book. I can see how all this should be all right from the dyed-in-the-wool shopkeeper point of view. The store is full of goody-goody girls and men—full of them: people who have been foully taught about sex, about motherhood, about the body. It is easy to see what Leaves of Grass must look like to people with such eyes. The Leaves do not need any excuse; they need to be understood. If I did not understand them I would dislike them myself, God knows! But all this fear of indecency, all this noise about purity and sex and the social order . . . is nasty—too nasty to make any compromise with.

May 3, 1888

How people reel when I say father-stuff and mother-stuff and onanist and bare legs and belly! O God! you might suppose I was citing some diabolical obscenity.

December 17, 1888

Children of Adam stumps the worst and the best: I have even tried hard to see if it might not as I grow older or experience new moods stump me: I have even almost deliberately tried to retreat. But it would not do. When I tried to take those pieces out of the scheme the whole scheme came down about my ears.

March 28, 1888

It takes some time to get accustomed to me, but if the folks will only persevere they will finally feel right comfortable in my presence. Children of Adam—the poems—are very innocent: they will not shake down a house.

June 25, 1888

I claim to be altogether radical—that's my chief stock in trade: take the radicalism out of the Leaves—do you think anything worth while would be left?

May 23, 1888

I am well satisfied with my success with titles—with Leaves of Grass, for instance, though some of my friends themselves rather kicked against it at the start—particularly the literary hair-splitters, who rejected it as a species of folly. "Leaves of Grass," they said: "there are no *leaves* of grass; there are *spears* of grass: that's your word, Walt Whitman: spears, spears." But *Spears* of Grass would not have been the same to me. Etymologically *leaves* is correct —scientific men use it so. I stuck to leaves, leaves, leaves, until it was able to take care of itself. Now it has got well started on its voyage—it will never be displaced.

May 20, 1888

I can see the necessity in some cases of extensive advertising, giving: some books depend for their sale on making a devil of a racket: but my book is of another order: it is the collected statement of my life—of my work: a statement of what I signify in the literary, the American, firmament, if anything: it will be taken that way or not at all: it is in a way my good-bye—to be recognized as such after I am gone.

March 25, 1889

LETTERS & LETTER WRITING

W. loves to receive letters—any letters, provided they are in the true sense human documents. He is always disappointed if the postman passes without stopping. This evening, while we talked, Mrs. Davis stuck her head in at the doorway and W. quickly asked: "Any letters?" "No, not one." "Not one? Not one? That's bad luck."

April 26, 1888

••••••••••••••••••

I like these letters from people I don't know, from people who don't know me, these confessions of love, these little "how do you dos" that appear every now and then out of mysterious obscure places.

April 19, 1888

I get confessions every now and then: from women, from men: they seem to inure to the kind of work I do: I don't as a rule know what to do with them: they mainly amaze me.

February 24, 1889

That men, women, we never meet, have not even heard of, except in the accidental way, should respond to our work—that is a thing to be pondered. It's a waft of something, a scent, a flavor, some indefinable entity, that must not be carelessly regarded or passed by.

January 21, 1889

People often sit down to write letters much as the professional author sits down to work: they have nothing to say but say a great deal about saying nothing.

July 21, 1888

John [Burroughs] writes letters—real letters. He does not strike you as a maker of phrases. I get so many letters that are distinctly literary—written for effect—labored over —worked upon to be made just so, just so: every phrase nicely balanced—all the words in place. John has the real art—the art of succeeding by not trying to succeed: he is the farmer first, the man, before he is the writer: that is the key . . .

July 3, 1888

Is there anything better in literature than the best letters?

August 21, 1888

Didn't you like his letter? It was very warm—very comfortable: like a fire for your backbone when you go in out of the cold.

July 30, 1888

. . . it was a letter full of good feeling—containing a remembrance of my birthday . . . a handsome remembrance, of money. It was a letter that went straight to my heart,—you know the heart is often reached through the pocket!

May 28, 1889

I was never a fulsome correspondent myself—wrote no superfluous letters: wrote very deliberately: often made a draft of my notes. I rarely do that now—very few people do it—except, of course, in official and business circles. . . . It involved a lot of useless work—made a man a slave: a long letter was half a day's job: God! I used to sweat over it even in cold weather.

June 13, 1888

I don't believe I ever wrote a purely literary letter—ever got discussing books or literary men or writers or artists of any sort in letters: the very idea of it makes me sick. I like letters to be personal—very personal—and then stop.

May 11, 1888

LIFE

7.30 P.M. Found Harned at W.'s with Corning, candidate for the pulpit of the Unitarian church on Benson Street. . . . W. asked Corning: "And what may be the subject of your sermon tomorrow?" "My subject? Why—the tragedy of the ages." "And what may be the tragedy of the ages?" "The crucifixion." "What crucifixion?" "The crucifixion of Jesus, of course." "You call that the tragedy of the ages?" "Yes—what do you call it?" "It is a tragedy. But *the* tragedy? O no! I don't think I would be willing to call it *the* tragedy." "Do you know any tragedy that meant so much to man?" "Twenty thousand tragedies—all equally significant." "I'm no bigot—I don't think I make any un- reasonable fuss over Jesus—but I never looked at the thing the way you do." "Probably not. But do it now—just for once. Think of the other tragedies, just for once: the tragedies of the average man—the tragedies of every-day— the tragedies of war and peace—the obscured, the lost, tragedies: they are all cut out of the same goods. I think too much is made of the execution of Jesus Christ. I know Jesus Christ would not have approved of this himself: he knew that his life was only another life, any other life, told

big; he never wished to shine, especially to shine at the
general expense. Think of the other tragedies, the twenty
thousand, just for once, Mr. Corning."

May 5, 1888

....

The common heroisms of life are anyhow the real
heroisms; the impressive heroisms: not the military kind,
not the political kind: just the ordinary world kind, the bits
of brave conduct happening about us: things that don't get
into the papers—things that the preachers don't thank God
for in their pulpits—the real things, nevertheless—the only
things that eventuate in a good harvest.

April 20, 1888

I am never convinced by the formal martyrdoms alone: I
see martyrdoms wherever I go: it is an average factor in
life: why should I go off emotionally half-cocked only about
the ostentatious cases?

October 15, 1888

I am not a saint—have never been guilty of setting up
for a saint. I find some of my friends—some of the ardent
eulogists—making very many claims for me which I would
not make for myself. Neither do I feel that I am such an
awful sinner: I have made mistakes—many of them: led
an average human life: not too good, not too bad—just
a so-so sort of life. I don't spend much time wondering
whether I should not have been better or might not have
been worse.

October 30, 1888

I never, never was troubled to know whether I would be saved or lost: what was that to me?

January 9, 1889

. . . my ought-to-have-been, like most of the ought-to-have-beens, is upset, made light of, scattered, put to rout, by what is: the what-ares are harder to contend with than the ought-to-have-beens.

November 10, 1888

I don't spend much of my time with regrets for anything: yet sometimes I regret that I never went to Europe: other times I regret that I never learned to read German and French. No doubt it's all just as well as it is: it all came about according to what they describe as "the ordinances of God": there's no chance in it: maybe I'd have been modified if I had ever broken loose from my accustomed ways—become a traveller, become a linguist: that might have meant harm to the Leaves: my destiny seems to have been to live my whole life here in America without any untoward interruptions.

February 2, 1889

We must not look back over our shoulders at the world: we should meet each day as it comes with the same assumption: we can make each new day the best of days if we get the habit.

March 7, 1889

. . . one of my chief doctrines, which is, that we should never become so absorbed in the ornamental occupations as to lose connection with life. Some men lead professional

Whitman about 1871

lives—some men just live: I prefer to just live. I never want to be thought to be contending that any amount of isolated esthetic achievement can compensate for the loss of the comrade life of the world: the comrade life, the right life of the one in the crowd, which is of all human ideals the most to be desired, the only one to be finally desired, and perpetuated.

September 1, 1888

. . . why my life? why any life? No life is a failure. I have done the work: I have thrown my life into the work: in those early years: teaching, loafing, working on the newspapers: travelling: then in Washington—clerking, nursing the soldiers: putting it up for what it was worth: into the book—pouring it into the book: honestly, without stint, giving the book all, all, all: why should I call it a failure? why? why? I don't think a man can be so easily wrecked as that.

December 18, 1888

I did a lot of . . . work in the hospitals: it was in a sense the most nearly real work of my life. Books are all very well but this sort of thing is so much better—as life is always better than books—as life in life is always superior to life in a book.

July 8, 1888

I suppose the best plan is to have no plan—to keep fluid, to let the influences possess you for what they may: of course you want to know in general where you're going, but apart from that I doubt if trying to live life on some mathematical basis can help a man to fulfil himself.

January 1, 1889

All my life here, is made up of pathetically little things: yet I don't know but all life is more or less like that—made dear or cheap to us in the proportion that we can accommodate ourselves to the kind of people we must meet, the kind of meals we must eat, the kind of clothes we must wear, the kind of pleasures we must have. We may make an adventure abroad occasionally, but for the main part the little motives become the big forces in existence.

February 14, 1889

After all, "nothing" makes up a good deal of a man's life: these trifles are registers, explanations, confirming, justifying.

November 20, 1888

It is surprising how little a man may live on if he must: live not meanly but with about all that is needed to make him comfortable . . .

May 23, 1888

It is always my point—don't submit to provocations, irritabilities, black fancies of the superficial day: go your way unmoved—on and on to what you are required to do: the rest will take care of itself.

September 4, 1888

We must be resigned, but not too much so: we must be calm, but not too calm: we must not give in—yet we must give in some: that is, we must grade our rebellion and our conformity—both.

March 6, 1889

. . . it looks easy to regulate a man from the outside:
but every life has to be lived from the inside after all . . .

February 16, 1889

What a thing is habit! . . . Curiously, it is harder to
break away from your vices than from your virtues: sometimes it seems easier to go to the Devil than to go to God!

August 13, 1888

It is a study—a profound study—the play in life as much
as the work in life. . . . Sometimes you don't pay too much
for play if you pay your last cent for it.

August 5, 1888

That's all there is in life for people—just to grow near
together.

May 17, 1888

. . . the story of the old woman . . . she insisted that
every woman born, man born, had his or her mate, somewhere—if they could but find out where! I suppose that
should be the whole matter of life—the whole story: to
find the mate, the environment—what to be,—then, adjust-
ment.

August 17, 1889

....

LIKES & DISLIKES

....

In at W.'s at 7.45, evening. W. lying on bed. Inclined to chat—speaking at ease. I let him go on. He hates questions.

July 9, 1888

....

I like to cross-examine, but I don't like to be cross-examined.

May 5, 1888

I am not fond of being catechized—indeed rather run from it: I am not fond of questions—any questions, in short, that require answers.

May 20, 1888

I like the outright person—the hater, the lover—the unmistakable yes or no: the street "damn you!" or "how are you me boy?"

June 8, 1888

I am afraid of the man who apologized for his opposition.

June 2, 1888

I like to get all my relations with people personal, human. I hate to think I can possibly excite any professional feeling in another.

August 4, 1888

I hate to think of myself as pensive, despondent, melancholy.

December 24, 1888

I have very little liking for deliberate wits—for men who start out, with malice prepense, to be funny—just as I should distrust deliberate pathos—the fellow who sets out to be serious, to shed tears, or make others.

August 24, 1889

I don't like afternoon performances—never did—they seem very impropitious.

August 6, 1889

If there's anything I like less than gratitude it's ingratitude.

September 10, 1888

. . . respectability has no use for me: I suppose the distaste is mutual.

April 6, 1889

....

LITERARY INDIVIDUALS

....

Much cooler today. W. more comfortable though still weak. Sat up and read and wrote some, but "irregularly, in snatches." Towards evening started reading the plate proofs. . . . "If we keep pegging away slowly but persistently, the book must in the end come out—if I should last, and I guess I will. But we musn't crow until we've left the last limit of the woods behind us—till we're clean out into the open. The vicissitudes are many—the certainties few. I have got beyond the point where I make the least calculation for the morrow—for any morrow. Yet it is our chief business to plod ahead, not disturbed, frittered away, with thoughts of things that might be. . . ."

W. said to me tonight: "Beware of the literary cliques —keep well in the general crowd: beware of book sympathies, caste sympathies."

August 19, 1888

....

A literary class in America always strikes me with a laugh or with nausea . . .

August 8, 1888

I do not value literature as a profession. I feel about literature what Grant did about war. He hated war. I hate literature. I am not a literary West Pointer: I do not love a literary man as a literary man, as a minister of a pulpit loves other ministers because they are ministers: it is a means to an end, that is all there is to it: I never attribute any other significance to it.

April 22, 1888

It seems to me that all real authorship is manhood—that my sympathy for manhood includes authorship even if it don't make authorship a preferred object of worship. What is authorship in itself if you cart it away from the main stream of life? It is starved, starved: it is a dead limb off the tree—it is the unquickened seed in the ground.

August 19, 1888

The big fellows are always the generous fellows: they recognize each other wherever they are. It's the generosity that makes the big fellow. It will do for the little crowd to have all the bickerings, the mean jealousies, the quarreling ambitions, the mean policies. And you know that's the way to distinguish the little from the big. The thing we call smart, clean, skilful—that thing is not big. Those who regard literature as an exercise, a plaything, a joke, a display, are not big—they are small of the small. There's nothing so riles me as this exhibition of professional acquirement.

June 8, 1888

There are a thousand and one gnats, mosquitoes, camp-followers, hanging about the literary army, and each of 'em thinks he must have a fling at Walt Whitman. They know nothing about him—maylike never read or even looked at his book—but that's no matter: that, in fact, seems to be taken as a special qualification for their carpings and crowings.

August 31, 1888

I am not literary: it is as a man that I should wish to be accepted, if at all—judged.

November 22, 1888

Most literary men, as you know, are the kind of men a hearty man would not go far to see . . .

January 16, 1889

Literary men learn so little from life—borrow so much from the borrowers.

April 24, 1888

....

LITERATURE

....

W. said: "I have this afternoon mailed two pieces to the Herald—two more throws against oblivion." I laughed— W. adding: "It does seem funny. A man makes a pair of shoes—the best—he expects nothing of it: he knows they will wear out: that's the end of the good shoe, the good man. Any kind of a scribbler writes any kind of a poem and

expects it to last forever. Yet the poems wear out, too—
often faster than the shoes. . . ."

April 28, 1888

....

Literature is big only in one way—when used as an aid
in the growth of the humanities—a furthering of the cause
of the masses—a means whereby men may be revealed to
each other as brothers.

June 8, 1888

I find nothing in literature that is valuable simply for its
professional quality: literature is only valuable in the measure of the passion—the blood and muscle—with which it is
invested—which lies concealed and active in it.

July 14, 1888

. . . the *grand* does not appeal to me: I dislike the simply *art* effect—art for art's sake, like literature for literature's sake, I object to, not, of course, on prude grounds,
but because literature created on such a principle (and art
as well) removes us from humanity, while only from humanity in mass can the light come.

April 26, 1888

The story writers do not as a rule attract me. . . .
What do you make of them?—what is their future significance? Have they any? Don't they just come and go—don't
they just skim about, butterfly about, daintily, in fragile
literary vessels, for awhile—then bow their way out?

April 28, 1888

As a general thing I don't enjoy dialect literature: it's rather troublesome stuff to handle . . . but though I don't care much for the dialect writers myself I acknowledge their validity, value, pertinence: that some of them are remarkably gifted: they indicate, stand for, exemplify, an important phase in our literary development.

February 23, 1889

Do you suppose I accept the almost luny worship of Shakespeare—the cult worship, the college-chair worship? Not a bit of it—not a bit of it. I do not think Shakespeare was the all in all of literature. I think there were twenty thousand things coming before him and at his time and since —things, men, illuminati—and everything has to be counted. Shakespeare was the greatest of his kind—but how about his kind?

May 11, 1888

LOAFING

"So far as good meals and a relish of them would prove," said W., as evening wore on, "this has been for me a better day—a best day altogether." Said he was getting "venturesome," enjoying "high hopes of a positive rally." "But," he wound up with saying, "we had better not brag." . . .

I had been out on the Wissahickon with Anne Mont-

gomerie. "That reminds me," said W., "that years ago I
thought some of pitching my own tent out there—squat-
ting—loafing the rest of my days in that vicinity. I cannot
be said even now to have wholly given up the idea: though
I don't suppose that it matters much where I happen to
spend the rest of my days. And you are right, too, Horace,
about abandon—the giving in to the hour—steering clear
of mental botheration—particularly of the botheration how
to be good and all that. Oh! I love that beautiful country
—that long road along the creek—even the very fence—
(the long lines of the fence up hill and down—the rugged,
knotty lines): some of my happiest hours have been spent
there—some of my freest hours."

July 15, 1888

....

I find the best way to spend my days—at least did long
ago—is the free way: not to make plans, but to go this path
or that as the mood dictates.

July 29, 1888

I can easily see that is one way—indeed, not only a good
way, but who knows but *the* way?—as, for one to take a
walk—allured by a tree, a bush, a stream, a mountain, a
sky: just freely, when and as the spirit dictates, not as I put
it, by *malice prepense*. My friends could never understand
me, that I would start out so evidently without design for
nowhere and stay long and long.

February 14, 1889

My own favorite loafing places have always been the
rivers, the wharves, the boats—I like sailors, stevedores.
I have never lived away from a big river.

August 1, 1888

Photograph of Whitman by Frank Pearsall about 1872, autographed five years later

An old wharf, the decayed, rotted soaked, beams, pilings: the debris: the grass-grown—mossy endings, surfaces —oh! they appeal to me most of all.

September 9, 1889

As I am fond of saying, no man will willingly abdicate his own dung hill. Allowing for all else, what can return to him the price of freedom but freedom?

April 27, 1889

....

LOVE & FRIENDSHIP

....

2.30 P.M. W. sitting in his usual place. Neither reading nor writing—yet not dozing: hands folded across his stomach—seeming to be lost in thought. Particularly affectionate somehow to-day. Some of his mail down by his feet: letter and paper for Bucke: spoke of these. "I finished my letter, as I told you, last night: put it up: there it is: and The Critic, too: I think he will like to receive that: Maurice has a curious affinity for all the odds and ends Whitmanesque." . . .

It commenced to snow about noon: now snowing hard and lying: the first snow storm practically of the season. W. asked: "Was it not unusually light early this morning?" Then: "I woke unusually early: it seemed to me the light came through the slats there piercingly: I wondered if it

were in some way from an artificial light." We talked of
the river: how the river is on days like this: W. interro-
gating. I was to go to Germantown in the late afternoon.
"Ah!" and after a slight wait: "Well, if you meet out there
with any inquiring friends, tell them Walt Whitman sends
his best love. . . .

". . . I think there is nothing beyond the comrade—the
man, the woman: nothing beyond: even our lovers must be
comrades: even our wives, husbands: even our fathers, mothers: we can't stay together, feel satisfied, grow bigger, on
any other basis."

January 20, 1889

••••••••••••••••••

. . . the good comrades are not all dead yet: look at
the fellows who are turning up here all the time from every
quarter of the globe: the world is as rich in comradeship as
ever—is always renewed: if we do nothing to invite the
new comrades we must not be surprised if they do not come.

March 7, 1889

. . . in a sense I have had a varied life: if having very
bitter enemies and friends very sweet—a good taste of both
—is variety, then I have had it.

April 6, 1889

I've had good friends as well as good enemies: a man
who has had the friends I have had can afford to forget
that he has enemies.

May 27, 1888

I don't believe any man ever lived who was more fortunate in the friendship of good women. I don't mean respectable women, so-called—I mean good women.

June 14, 1888

I guess friendship is constitutional, or in great part so— you like cabbage or you don't and that's all there is about it.

July 11, 1888

Most of my friends have been thinkers—people of the highest, though not of the professional, poetic nature. The great literary leaders—most of them—had no idea that I could be taken seriously and refused to condone my existence. If God Almighty was willing to be responsible for me, well and good: but as for them—they would have no Walt Whitman: their skirts were clean.

October 7, 1888

If I keep on in this way I shall by and by have a Hebrew clientage—and I do not see why I should not—I see every reason why I should: for am I not a Biblical fellow myself—born and bred in Hebrewism—the old forerunners, teachers, prophets? And all my Hebrew friends are turning out to be among the young—you would call that an omen, wouldn't you?

July 14, 1889

They may be wrong in what they say of my book but they are not wrong in their love: love is never wrong.

July 7, 1888

It seems to be the notion of some people that I should "select" my friends—accept and reject and so forth. Love, affection, never selects—just loves, is just affectionate.

May 9, 1888

Any love that involves slavery is a false love—any love.

May 28, 1888

....

METHOD

....

2 P.M. Last night W. told me he had not felt up to going over the plate proofs. I went home and worked until two o'clock on them. . . . Worked again until eleven this morning. Now submit them to W. He sat reading the Century as I entered. "So it's Horace again?" Looked rather well. How was he? "Not a bit nifty—not a bit nifty," he replied. Nifty? what was nifty? "Did you never hear that colloquialism—nifty?—n-i-f-t-y—sassy, on edge?" Continued: "I have sat about here, have read some, have dozed more—that is the history of the day." . . . We examined the proofs together. Very particular in certain details. . . . He objected to some changes I suggested. . . . "That puts us in good shape," he said after we had finished our job together. . . .

He further said: "You find me cautious. . . ." "You are willing to take time enough to get the right time."

"That's a mighty good way to say it: yes, time enough: I never fire my gun before I cock it—I never cock it until I know just exactly the game I am after." "That is, you have discovered that you're no good in a quick charge but a sure thing in a long siege." W. looked at me fixedly: "That's damned clever, Horace: but look out—you musn't get yourself in the habit of saying clever things—it's a dangerous practice—lands many a man many a time in a lie. Still, it happens that this clever thing is also true, so I forgive you. Yes, I have made the best of my sluggish pulse by trying to keep it sure, strong. Every man has to learn his own best method: my method is to go slow, extra slow. All great work is cautious work—is done with an eye on all the horizons of the spirit: in the absence of such gravity we become dabblers—the big things don't get said, don't get done."

September 2, 1888

....

I always keep to my own method—to write as moved to write, and what: and what depends upon the moment.

August 9, 1889

I never start out bent upon doing anything by a particular method but let events grow their own way.

September 2, 1888

The idea must always come first—is indispensable. Take my own method—if you can call it that. I have the idea clearly and fully realized before I attempt to express it. Then I let it go. The idea becomes so important to me I may perhaps underrate the other element—the expressional element—that first, last and all the time emphasis placed by literary men on the mere implement of words instead of upon the work itself.

April 24, 1888

I have feelings about things, nothing more. I try and try and try again, and then try all over if necessary, until the approvable result is secured. I could not tell how to get it, but I can recognize my own when it appears.

July 4, 1888

That has mainly been my method: I have caught much on the fly: things as they come and go—on the spur of the moment. I have never forced my mind: never driven it to work: when it tired, when writing became a task, then I stopped: that was always the case—always my habit.

November 21, 1888

I don't revise my revisions too much—polish: I don't hold it to be principally important to develope special technical flavors. Studying for recitation is mainly technical—tends to reaction: encourages formalism. I keep as far away from the mere machinery of composition as I can.

September 9, 1888

I have never given any study merely to expression: it has never appealed to me as a thing valuable or significant in itself: I have been deliberate, careful, even laborious: but I have never looked for finish—never fooled with technique more than enough to provide for simply getting through: after that I would not give a twist of my chair for all the rest.

November 12, 1888

I have suffered all my life from the misjudgments of people who looked with suspicion upon all I do. I am not concerned to please them, but I am anxious to come to conclusions satisfactory to my own soul. My ways are very methodical: I have been much criticised for that: but my ways are mine and are necessary to me. I need to isolate myself—to work along very undemonstrative lines: I can never rush: I must proceed in a leisurely manner as if I have all the time there is.

October 31, 1888

I am for caution—for never claiming too much—for always allowing for a beyond.

September 10, 1888

....

MUSIC

....

6.50 P.M. Went down with Morris Lychenheim, intending to pick Ed up and go to the opera together. W. in his bedroom when we arrived. We talked there about 20 minutes. He very courteously showed L. to a seat and remembered the book he had signed for him. At one point asked, "So you came down to take Ed along?" Then spoke of operas—of this one "The Chimes of Normandy," he "knew nothing" and asked, "Can you tell me about it?" Adding, "Somehow, nobody can tell me!" But we should get a book of "the scheme." "In my opera days, I always took care to get a libretto the day before, then took care to leave it at home on the day itself!"

August 7, 1889

■■■■■■■■■■■■■■■■■

I looked upon these concerts in the open air—the nights often so beautiful, calm—as bright gleams athwart the sad history of that harrowing city and time. Yet my enjoyment was altogether untechnical: I knew nothing about music: simply took it in, enjoyed it, from the human side: had a good ear—did not trouble myself to explain or analyze.

January 11, 1889

My younger life was so saturated with the emotions, raptures, up-lifts, of such musical experiences that it would be surprising indeed if all my future work had not been colored by them. A real musician running through Leaves of Grass—a philosopher musician—could put his finger on this and that anywhere in the text no doubt as indicating the activity of the influences I have spoken of.

August 21, 1888

■■■

NATURE

■■■

7.15 P.M. W. writing a postal. Shook hands, then went on writing. Ed in the meantime coming in and waiting. W. handed Ed two postals and two wrapped papers. Ed went to the post office. Spoke of his health—said that he still feels comparatively well. . . .

W. had another letter for me. He picked it up from the accustomed place on the table. "It's from Rossetti," he said: "I've been reading it over: William Rossetti: full of wise and beautiful things—overflowing with genial winsome good will: you'll feel its treasurable quality." I sat there and read. He said: "Read it aloud: I can easily enjoy it again." When I got to the passage describing the walks W. interrupted me: "Oh! that's so fine—so fine, fine, fine: he brings back my own walks to me . . . they make me hungry, tied up as I am now and for good in a room: hungry: hungry. Horace, do you sometimes feel the earth hunger? the desire for the dirt? to get out doors, into the woods, on the roads? to roll in the grass: to cry out: to play tom fool with yourself in the free fields? . . ."

November 20, 1888

. . . .

. . . the great thing for one to do when he is used up, is to go out to nature—throw yourself in her arms—submit to her destinies.

August 22, 1889

Nature has a keen way of putting its strength out: if a man lack in one sense, nature puts that strength—the strength due that—into another.

December 23, 1888

I have been watching them for an hour—they are rarely beautiful—vast, deep, slatey masses, hurrying across the sky, chasing one another. See those now!—how they go and go, tireless and without number. It has always been

one of my finer joys, to watch the varied, varying, ever-
changing, inter-locking, cloud-shapes!

June 26, 1889

The masters keep on coming and coming again: nature
can always do better than her best: is prodigal, exhaustless.

August 10, 1888

NEWSPAPERS

Morning, 11.15 W. just done breakfast. Had slept later
than usual. . . . W. said: "It was only half-sleep, however, all night." Sat in the chair. Hair rather in disorder.
Pale. Eyes languid and weary. Talked clearly but as if with
strain. Said instantly to me: "Sit down: sit down on the sofa
over there"—then asked: "It is a good deal colder this morning?"—feeding a few bits of wood to the fire at the same
moment. Ate some toast. Musgrove came in and handed
W. the Press.* He said: "I have eaten little: there was
little to stimulate me to eat." I said: "I'm afraid the Press
won't do much towards stimulating you: it's full of tariff
this morning." W. returned: "I supposed so. . . . The
Press is of all the papers I know the meanest, most malignant, most lying—a searcher after hidden blackness, a sus-

---

* *Philadelphia Press,* a newspaper founded in 1857, merged with the
Philadelphia Public Ledger in 1920. W. T.

picioner of motives, a pecker at the foibles of humanity: a
sort of journalistic imp of Beelzebub." I laughed. "My—
your sleep must have been a soothing one!" He laughed
with me. "Well, Horace—that was maybe going it pretty
strong even on the very nasty Press, but it does make me
mad as a hornet every time I look at it." Then I asked:
"Hasn't it stimulated you after all? It has brought the red
back into your face!" He nodded: "That's certainly a
cheerful way to look at it, Horace: I may after all have
something to thank even the Press for."

September 30, 1888

....

The Press: the most ignominious of all ignominious examples of what a decent newspaper should not be! I cannot
account for the fact that I read it day after day except by
the thought that I haven't energy enough to stop it: the
Press: the most venomous, the most trivial, of all the so-
called organs of public opinion: an illustration *par excellence* of the evil possibilities of journalism: to me the ideal
of the traitorous, the superficial, the gross, the low—yet
with a certain almost impressive brazenness of demeanor.

April 3, 1889

There is a whole host of writers for the press—there
always have been a host of 'em, though never, I think, so
wholesale in their methods as now—to whom the truth was
of no account, to whom the only things of account were, to
create interest and get pay for it!

April 22, 1889

I interest the newspaper men as one of the strange fellows—they look for freakish characters—it is among these

I come in. How few of them—of all of them—actors, writers, professional men, laborers—on whom you can't put a tag.

June 29, 1888

According to the papers I am crazy, dead, paralyzed, scrofulous, gone to pot in piece and whole: I am a wreck from stem to stern—I am sour, sweet—dirty, clean—taken care of, neglected: God knows what I am, what I am not. The American newspaper beats the whole world telling the truth, the whole truth and nothing but the truth!

June 15, 1888

It seems to be a penalty a man has to pay, even for very little notoriety—the privilege of being lied about. Yet I rest the case finally on the good sense of my friends—their knowledge that, of printed matter anyhow, fully half—three-quarters perhaps—even a greater proportion, is lie—is admitted to be such.

May 6, 1889

By some curious mischance, newspapers have the faculty of sending to you, fellows who put down what you do not say, but carefully avoid giving a word of what you do.

May 30, 1889

....

PEOPLE

....

We found ourselves talking of the spontaneities—how some of the most beautiful things happen without a plan. I spoke of the driver of a wagon on the Chestnut Street hill by the river: "his horse fell down—could not get up: a dozen men as by one instinct rushed into the street— gave the carter a boost, got the horse safely on his feet: all then laughingly going their ways again: no scheme, no reward: just the finer human impulse at play." W. was immensely moved. "How splendid that is! That is wonderfully à propos: there are more cases like it than we can count. . . . There is always a manifest streak of good side by side with the bad. . . . I had a visitor—a Quaker lady—to-day. . . . She was here but shortly—explained that she had been out a while since, called on a friend: while waiting in the parlor had hit upon November Boughs on the table there: she had read . . . said that simply seeing that much had created in her the desire to see more. . . . She did not stay long: was mindful of what had been told her down stairs. When she came to go she took my hand, put into it a little folded piece of paper—so"—indicating: "said, 'Don't open it till I'm gone—this is not for thee alone but for me': passed out. When I looked, lo! she had left me a two dollar and a half gold piece. The whole manner of it was characteristic: much the way of the Friends. It is a singular feature in men, that to simply con-

fess a love is not enough: there must be some concrete
manifestation of it."

November 30, 1888

••••••••••••••••••

There's something in the human critter which only needs
to be nudged to reveal itself: something inestimably elo-
quent, precious: not always observed: it is a folded leaf:
not absent because we fail to see it: the right man comes—
the right hour; the leaf is lifted.

November 30, 1888

Have you noticed that the time to look for the best
things in best people is the moment of their greatest need?

September 26, 1888

I trust humanity: its instincts are in the main right: it
goes false, it goes true, to its interests, but in the long run
it makes advances. Humanity always has to provide for
the present moment as well as for the future: that is a
tangle, however you look at it. Why wonder, then, that humanity falls down every now and then? There's one thing
we have to remember—that the race is not free (free of
its own ignorance)—is hardly in a position to do the best
for itself: when we get a real democracy, as we will by and
bye, this humanity will have its chance—give a fuller report
of itself.

May 15, 1888

I am not a witness for saviors—exceptional men: for the
nobility—no: I am a witness for the average man, the
whole.

May 29, 1888

Whitman about 1872. Charles E. Feinberg Collection

What a poor miserable critter man is! A joker—a great joker for his little time: then nature comes along, buffets him once or twice, gives him two or three knocks: nature, the strong, the irresistible, the great bear: then what is man? where is the joker?

December 15, 1888

The largest part of our human tragedies are humanly avoidable: they come from greed, from carelessness, from causes not castastrophic, elemental: with more radical good heart most of our woes would disappear.

April 1, 1889

. . . I never admit that men have any troubles which they cannot eventually outgrow.

July 11, 1888

I suppose that under whatever conditions, we would have botherations—the race would have its struggles, trials, growls, doubts, horrors: all it now asked for achieved, it would solicit more—more and more: the human critter is just that sort of a being—and best so, no doubt.

April 12, 1889

There is no use hiding it from ourselves: there is a strain of slipperiness in the human critter: we all pray to be delivered from it: it is perhaps in some measure in all of us.

March 22, 1889

. . . we must recollect, man is such a scamp, such a wickedee—so essentially an ignoramm—that it is hard often to stand him—yet it is but right that the scamp should be represented.

May 26, 1889

. . . there seems to be the spice of the gambler in all of us: we'd do anything to get out of the beaten track—even commit crimes!

February 9, 1889

I have seen in the later years of my life exemplifications of devilishness, venom, in the human critter which I could not have believed possible in my more exuberant youth—a great lump of bad with the good.

July 11, 1888

Elite or not—put them at a ball and put some liquor in them and it's all one.

May 3, 1889

. . . take whiskey from a man as he is constituted now, and he will take absinthe, hasheesh.

April 13, 1889

I don't accept the temperance advocate so-called—neither do I accept the rum seller: I often say to them—hatchel each other all you can—I shan't grieve over it! But then aside from any feeling of that sort that I may have I remember that men are not to be made moral by violent means—by being spurred this way and that and told: "You shall do so and so and so!" Resolved, that men shall no longer lie, shall no longer steal, shall no longer commit adultery! As a matter of fact I am at times disposed to think that men are so because they are so—that no absence of saloons could in itself prevent them from going to the bad, to the devil, if you've a mind to put it that way: they go or don't go from an impulse within themselves or the want of it. Salvation can't be legislated.

June 3, 1888

PHILOSOPHY

W. drove up to Harned's just after one. . . . After W. had got to his chair Harned started off to mix him his usual toddy but W. called him back. "Never mind the toddy today, Tom: I can't take it—it would finish me." W. was very pale—at dinner very abstemious. "I almost didn't get here," said W. "I feel damned bad today: some time before long I'll get one of these bad days and that'll be the end of me: then you fellows will have a funeral on your hands. Have you got a funeral ready?" W. laughed. . . . Corning said to W.: "I'd like to see you in a pulpit once." "Once, did you say? once? That's all it would be: I wouldn't last more than once but I'd make all the fur fly while I lasted!". . .

W. speaking of the idea of immortality, of the "fact" as he prefers to call it. . . . "What the world calls logic is beyond me: I only go about my business taking on impressions—reporting impressions—though sometimes I imag-

ine that what we see is superior to what we reason about—
what establishes itself in the age, in the heart, is finally the
only logic—can boast of the only real verification."

May 13, 1888

....

Of all things, I am most lacking in what is called defi-
niteness, in so far as that applies to special theories of life
and death. As I grow older I am more firmly than ever
fixed in my belief that all things tend to good, that no bad
is forever bad, that the universe has its own ends to subserve and will subserve them well. Beyond that, when it
comes to launching out into mathematics—tying philosophy
to the multiplication table—I am lost—lost utterly. Let
them all whack away—I am satisfied: if they can explain,
let them explain: if they can explain they can do more than
I can do.

August 1, 1888

The debate is like many others—inconclusive. I never
knew a controversy of this character—each side ready to
swear to its accuracy, full of the arrogance of learning,
equipped with book knowledge—to end in anything like a
settlement: the problem was always as wide open at the end
as at the start.

September 6, 1888

I seem to be right, you seem to be right: do you regard
that as being impossible?

February 4, 1889

We feel like saying to the metaphysicians and moralists:
hold your horses, keep them well in hand—you never know

when you've got to take a sharp turn-about! It's like in medicine—this year's dogma is tomorrow thrown away.

August 22, 1888

Whether it is constitutional or what not with me, I stand for the sunny point of view—stand for the joyful conclusions. This is not because I merely guess: it's because my faith seems to belong to the nature of things—is imposed, cannot be escaped: can better account for life and what goes with life than the opposite theory.

October 4, 1888

Cheer! Cheer! Is there anything better in this world anywhere than cheer—just cheer? Any religion better?— any art? Just cheer!

May 16, 1888

I am a great contender for the world as it is—the ill along with the good. Indeed, I am more and more persuaded that the ill, too, has its part to subserve—its important part— that if ill did not exist, it would be a hopeless world and we would all go to the bad.

June 8, 1889

After all, I suppose good and bad weather comes back to the question, how do we ourselves feel? If we are well all is well, and vice versa.

December 8, 1888

....

PICTURES

....

In with W. at 7.45 till 9.20. When I entered he lay at full
length on the sofa from which he at once arose. Upon my
protest he said: "No, it's all right: I was just thinking
whether I should not go over to the window again." I helped
him across the room. . . .

W. is very amiable towards the portrait hunters. He
gives them pretty nearly everything they ask. . . . W.
says: ". . . I give the painters all the rope they want: I
humor them every way I know. [John White] Alexander
came, saw—but did he conquer? I hardly think so. He was
here several times, struggled with me—but since he left
Camden I have heard neither of him nor of his picture. . . .
I am not sorry the picture was painted but I would be sorry
to have it accepted as final or even as fairly representing
my showdown. I am a bit surprised too—I thought Alexander would do better, considering his reputation. Tom Eakins
could give Alexander a lot of extra room and yet beat him
at the game. Eakins is not a painter, he is a force. Alexander
is a painter."

June 8, 1888

....

I am always subjected to the painters: they come here and
paint, paint, paint, everlastingly paint. I give them all the
aid and comfort I can—I put myself out to make it possible
for them to have their fling: hoping all the time that now

the right man has come, now the thing will be done completely once and for all and hereafter I can hood my face.

May 10, 1888

I am persuaded that my painter has not arrived. I know I have been successfully taken—taken in all sorts of habits and hours—but somehow there is an elusive quality which so far no one has caught.

May 26, 1889

I find I often like the photographs better than the oils— they are perhaps mechanical, but they are honest. The artists add and deduct: the artists fool with nature—reform it, revise it, to make it fit their preconceived notion of what it should be.

May 10, 1888

I have been photographed, photographed, photographed, until the cameras themselves are tired of me.

June 22, 1888

They have photographed me all ages, sizes, shapes: they have used me for a show-horse again and again and again: they make the pictures and sell them: but as for paying me —well, they don't worry about that . . .

October 7, 1888

. . . my red, florid, blooded, complexion—my gray dull eyes—don't consort well together: they require different trimmings: it is very hard to adjust the camera to both.

January 17, 1889

I doubt color photography: how can it ever be? There seem to be insuperable chemical difficulties in the way. Yet how can we doubt anything in this age?

June 8, 1888

The art [photography] is growing with strides and leaps: God knows what it will come to: some of the smart wide awake fellows even back in that Lincoln time had a knack of catching life on the run, in a flash, as it shifted, moved, evolved.

November 4, 1888

Pictures are partial—they give a dash of a man, a phase . . .

August 17, 1888

. . . the sort of picture useful in totaling a man but not a total in itself.

November 10, 1888

The human expression is so fleeting—so quick—coming and going—all aids are welcome.

September 3, 1889

···

PLEASURES

···

W. woke up this morning feeling bum, but rallied a little towards noon. Very close, oppressive, today. Sat in a chair eating some grapes when I entered (1.15 P.M.). "I have been frugal today." Then he added: "Sit down—get that chair and bring it here." He resumed eating his grapes. . . .

W. said to me: "I like your interest in sports—ball, chiefest of all—base-ball particularly: base-ball is our game: the American game: I connect it with our national character. Sports take people out of doors, get them filled with oxygen—generate some of the brutal customs (so-called brutal customs) which, after all, tend to habituate people to a necessary physical stoicism. We are some ways a dyspeptic, nervous set: anything which will repair such losses may be regarded as a blessing to the race. We want to go out and howl, swear, run, jump, wrestle, even fight, if only by so doing we may improve the guts of the people: the guts, vile as guts are, divine as guts are!"

September 16, 1888

·················

I believe in all that—in baseball, in picnics, in freedom: I believe in the jolly all-round time—with the parsons and the police eliminated.

June 5, 1888

. . . many, many a time have I enjoyed such crowds—experienced the thrill of the crowd: for what, from what, who can tell? I am at home in such places: I respond sensitively to the life of the street—its almost contagion: it seizes you in spite of yourself, even against your sympathies, your dreams . . .

November 7, 1888

My own greatest pleasure at Pfaff's * was to look on—to see, talk little, absorb. I never was a great discusser, anyway—never. I was much better satisfied to listen to a fight than take part in it.

July 3, 1888

There was a time—not long ago, either—when the mere pleasure of locomotion—of having my arms and legs going out of doors—was a joy to me.

April 28, 1888

I am an open air man: winged. I am also an open water man: aquatic. I want to get out, fly, swim—I am eager for feet again! But my feet are eternally gone.

May 5, 1888

I was never what you could call a skillful swimmer but was quite good. I always hugely enjoyed swimming. My forte was—if I can say it that way—in floating. I possessed almost unlimited capacity for floating on my back—for however long: could almost take a nap meanwhile . . . that is to say I was very much at home in the water. I never could

---

* Pfaff's Cellar, a tavern at 653 Broadway, near Bleecker Street, New York, well-known meeting place of artists and writers in the 1850s. W. T.

do any of the surprising stunts of the other boys when I was young but I was a first-rate aquatic loafer.

July 20, 1888

Some people need harmless enthusiasms: better zest, ardor, warmth, decision, than nothing—than merely colorless inanity: better misapplied heat than no heat at all.

May 12, 1888

. . . enthusiasm: without that what is a man?

March 15, 1889

The wonderful new babies! Oh! how fully I entered into them! It used to be my delight to get the youngsters, the very young ones, take them in my arms, walk them—often sing to them—hours and hours and hours. I don't know who got the most joy out of it—it seems to me the baby's could never have equalled mine: the wonderful alluring babies!

May 9, 1889

I was up, it was near midnight: I felt a gnawing something here—a void—so I took some of the cakes [sent by Traubel's sister] and ate them alone, in the dark, in the dead silence. How much (perhaps all) the value of a thing —your joy, satisfaction, with it—consists in having it just at the right time: it may be a trifle but it is opportune. That's the way it was with the cakes. A little something at the right time is better than much and running over at the wrong time.

May 8, 1888

POETRY

Evening. W. at home. Lying on the sofa in the parlor and complaining of ill health. . . . "But what's the use growling? Everything don't come my way but lots of things do." Talked for a long time recumbent. Then sat up and faced me. "Rhys was here yesterday and the day before: he has now gone to New York. He intends to take in Niagara . . . then home. . . . 'After I have seen Niagara, after having seen you,' Rhys said, 'I can fairly say I have been to America to some purpose.' That's what he says. . . .

"He is very interesting to me. We talked of the poetic lilt. Rhys insists on it: insists on it, come good or bad."

May 16, 1888

Well—the lilt is all right: yes, right enough: but there's something anterior—more imperative. The first thing necessary is the thought—the rest may follow if it chooses—may play its part—but must not be too much sought after. The two things being equal I should prefer to have the lilt present with the idea, but if I got down my thought and the rhythm was not there I should not work to secure it. I am very deliberate—I take a good deal of trouble with words: yes, a good deal: but what I am after is the content not the music of words. Perhaps the music happens—it does no harm: I do not go in search of it.

May 16, 1888

There's no difference between Homer and Virgil—oh no!—and yet there is every difference: there is, what is there?—nothing at all, people will say: but that nothing is everything—it is the whole gap between the fellow who sings because he is moved to, and the fellow who sets out deliberately to sing, and so sings!

June 25, 1889

They talk about form: poetic form: this tradition for sculpture, that for painting, another for the written word: form: complying to the dicta of professors, pedagogue, stylists, grammarians. Well—a man can do that and be crowned: then he can not do it and take his chances . . .

February 8, 1889

The trouble with most poems is that they are nothing but poems—all poetry, all literary, not in any way human.

August 15, 1888

After all, if a fellow is to write poetry the secret is—get in touch with humanity—know what the people are thinking about: retire to the very deepest sources of life—back, back, till there is no farther point to retire to.

September 19, 1888

If they call me no poet then no-poet it may be. I don't care what they call me—by one name or another name—it is all one—so that I produce the result—so that I get my word spoken and heard—maybe move men and women.

August 16, 1888

Photograph of Whitman by Brady, New York. Autographed

It is the very worst sort of logic to try a poem by rules of logic—to try to confirm a round world by square tests—to sit down and argue a poem out, out, out, to an end—yes, to death.

July 9, 1888

I never commit poems to memory—they would be in my way.

September 9, 1888

....

POLITICS & PARTY

....

8 P.M. W. not at first lively but melted out. Harned there. Asked me: "What do you know in our affairs?" . . .

Spoke of lack of excitement over the election: "I read things about it here and there but it is all of the hell-take-the-other-side order and I make nothing worth while out of it." Harned asked: "Do you read Blaine's * speeches?" W. replied quickly: "No indeed—I've got too much respect for the clock." Then he added gravely: "It's coming about that we need a new politics—something of the human to supplant the political order: and it will come, too—maybe not soon, maybe not for some time: but it will come—it

---

* James Gillespie Blaine (1830–1893), a founder of the Republican Party in Maine, congressman, senator, and secretary of state. W. T.

must come : without it our democracy will go to the devil—
nothing can save it.''

October 22, 1888

....

The working class is slow to learn—they are cheated,
swindled, robbed, pay all the piper's bills and hear none of
the music—yet go on year after year putting their robbers
back in Congress, in the legislatures—making them mayors
and what not.

August 10, 1888

The people are lethargic—let things go—suffer themselves to be milked and thrown away by a class of political
scoundrels—they are so patient, often so stupid—blind to
their own divine descent—but finally they revolt—are up in
arms—raise hell. Then look out! But they are so slow—so
slow! This year or some year the people will do some new
things for America—hardly this year—the soil is not yet
sufficiently prepared—but some year. I wish the people believed in themselves as much as I believe in them!

June 23, 1888

More than all else I enjoy the sight of rebellion—of men
who stand aside from parties (yes—I may say, from
churches, too—sects)—refuse to be labelled, rejecting any
name that may be offered them : the vast floating vote,
ready to nip things in season, to cast their weight where
most needed, at critical moments, with no formal pledge or
party alliance.

September 13, 1888

What do I want with practical politics? Most all the practical politics I see anywhere is practical villainy. . . . I am not looking to politics to renovate politics: I am looking to forces outside—the great moral, spiritual forces—and these stick to their work, through thick and thin, through the mire and the mirage, until the proper time, and then assume control. The best politics that could happen for our republic would be the abolition of politics.

April 6, 1888

No man can look into what we call party politics without seeing what a mockery it all is—how little either Democrats or Republicans know about essential truths.

November 4, 1888

I see that the real work of democracy is done underneath its politics: this is especially so now, when the conventional parties have both thrown their heritage away, starting from nothing good and going to nothing good: the Republican party positively, the Democratic party negatively, the apologists of the plutocracy. You think I am sore on the plutocracy? Not at all: I am out to fight but not to insult it: the plutocracy has as much reason for being as poverty—and perhaps when we get rid of the one we will get rid of the other.

April 6, 1888

. . . how contemptible is the enthusiasm of the average voter—his sad, sickening, distressing talk of "my man," "my man," "my man." Our politics need a big lift to some higher plane—a big lift: probably will not get it until some more important issues make the lift worth while.

June 26, 1888

We have in a sense been fortunate in our Presidents: no matter what their backgrounds may have been the Presidents after they become Presidents have borne themselves well—the whole line of them: carried themselves according to their lights. . . . We are too apt to pause with particulars: the Presidency has a significance, a meaning, broader, higher, than could be imparted to it by any individual however spacious, satisfying. There is no great importance attaching to Presidents regarding them simply as individuals put into the chair after a partisan fight: the Presidency stands for a profounder fact; consider that: detached from that it is an incumbrance indeed, not a lift, to the spirit. We need to enclose the principle of the Presidency in this conception: here is the summing up, the essence, the eventuation, of the will of sixty millions of people of all races, colors, origins, inextricably intermixed: for true or false the sovereign statement of the popular hope.

November 5, 1888

I went to Washington as everybody goes there prepared to see everything done with some furtive intention, but I was disappointed—pleasantly disappointed. I found the clerks mainly earnest, mainly honest, anxious to do the right thing—very hard working, very attentive. . . . Washington is corrupt—has its own peculiar mixture of evil with its own peculiar mixture of good—but the evil is mostly with the upper crust—the people who have reputations—who are better than other people.

May 13, 1888

I am troubled by the merely mercenary influences that seem to be let loose in current legislation: the hog let loose:

the grabber, the stealer, the arrogant honorable so and so:
but I still have my faith—in the end my faith prevails.

November 1, 1888

I hardly seem in line with the Republican party any more
—in fact, the Republican party is hardly in line with itself.
. . . I never had entire faith—now I have hardly any faith
at all. . . . When these institutions start to die they die
on—nothing stops the process. . . . A party may win elections and be defeated anyway. The Republican party as it
is constituted now might win twenty elections without a single moral victory: the moral victories are the only victories
that count.

June 17, 1888

The political class is too slippery for me—even its best
examples: I seem to be reaching for a new politics—for a
new economy: I don't know quite what, but for something.

May 4, 1888

The whole gang is getting beyond me: I find it harder
and harder every year to reconcile myself to the exhibit
they make: they narrow, narrow, narrow every year: after
awhile I'll be altogether without a political home unless I
build one for myself.

June 20, 1888

We've got a hell of a lot to learn yet before we're a real
democracy: we've gone beyond all the others, very far beyond some, but we're far from having yet achieved our
dream: we'll do it, after a hell of a lot of bellyaching,

retching—often making mistakes, committing crimes: we'll get there in the end: God knows we're not there yet.

March 31, 1889

....

PRIME OF LIFE

....

W. passed a good day in all respects except as to strength. Complains of appalling weakness. Wonderfully cheerful in the evening on my arrival, talking most freely for more than an hour. Little work done. Read some papers. Wrote notes. . . .

He asked me some questions about my health. "When you come in, each day, any time, when I ask you, as I always do: How have you been? your invariable answer is: Well, always well. Are you always so well? It is so great —so superb—to be always well. However, these are your years to expect it—from eighteen to forty-five—halcyon days, sure enough—and if there's anything in a man, physically or mentally, it's sure to come out, to give an account of itself, along through that stretch of life."

July 23, 1888

....

If we've got the stuff in us, if we're dead in earnest about it, it'll find its own way of getting out.

May 31, 1888

I can imagine no worse fortune for a man who amounts to anything, who hopes to grow and flower, who has in him the stuff of achievement, than to come into an income, ease, goods—be put into pawn to the world's patronage.

August 21, 1888

Our young men have a sneaking hunger for loaves and fishes: they look for fat berths—get them: settle down: they are under orders—they are to obey, obey: and so they succeed in destroying all their individuality.

May 16, 1888

Breaking loose is the thing to do: breaking loose, resenting the bonds, opening new ways: but when a fellow breaks loose or starts to or even only thinks he thinks he'll revolt he should be quite sure he knows what he has undertaken.

January 11, 1889

I remember when I was a young man one of my placards for remembrance—for every-day contemplation—was this: to not take a severe view of things—to guard lest I settle into the mood of the book-bookies, scholars, critics— growling at the *universe* in general and all its particulars. I think I have mainly succeeded in holding myself in check, if check were needed.

May 19, 1889

Time was when I had to say big things about myself in order to be honest with the world—in order to keep in a good frame of mind until the world caught up. A man has sometimes to whistle very loud to keep a stiff upper lip.

August 30, 1888

It is singular how soon some natures come to a head and how long it takes others to ripen, though I believe, as a rule, the slow fruit is the best.

August 22, 1888

. . . it's mainly the slow maturers who mature to stay— mature to grow.

January 1, 1889

I have heard it said that reason comes with the forties. I should say as to most men, that reason does not come even then—does not come at all—for I am impressed with the general lack of it.

August 31, 1888

. . . I am a great believer in every fellow's setting-to and doing what he feels he ought to do—following out the Quaker spirit; so if you must, you must!

June 24, 1889

······································

PRINTERS & PUBLISHERS

······································

7.15 P.M. W. lying on bed. Ed had told me downstairs that his condition was unchanged. It seemed really so. He said something to that effect at once. Once during my stay got up to urinate but could not. "The trouble seems to lie in the kidneys," he explained: "I am not relieved: the pain is intense: I am weak: have been lying here nearly all day." Dressed of course. . . .

While I sat there . . . I heard him fumbling in his pocket: he was after his purse. "I was thinking," he said, "I had half a dollar here, but I have not. Have you change for this?" extending me a dollar bill. After I had made the change he said to me: "I am wondering if the man over there at Oldach's who hit off the book so well to my taste should not be shaken hands with, congratulated: so you must give him this for me: tell him to go out to-morrow— take a glass of beer—some cheese—lunch—for me." Here he paused: then added: "He is a German, I suppose? anyhow I want him to have it." Suppose he is not a German? "Well—he'll know how to eat the lunch anyway." W. proceeded: "In business it is too much the custom to sink labor in money values: which is all the more reason why I should break through the custom—show that I put quite another estimate upon work, product."

December 2, 1888

················

The prospect of an early production of both books gives me a sense of relief beyond words. I want you to say to all the fellows—the printer men—all of them (be sure you don't forget the proof-reader) that Walt Whitman is grateful for everything they have done—that his pay is not the pay of money but the pay of love. Tell them that— tell even the flinty ones that. I want them to know that I am not in merely trade relations with them.

August 25, 1888

I want you to reach the workmen direct—treat with the craftsman without an intermediary—with the man who sets the type, the man who puts it into form, the man who runs the foundry: reach them, yes, with a dollar now and then.

May 25, 1888

I like to supervise the production of my own books: I have suffered a good deal from publishers, printers—especially printers, damn 'em, God bless 'em! The printer has his rod, which has often fallen on me good and powerful.

May 22, 1888

. . . having been a printer myself, I have what may be called an anticipatory eye—know pretty well as I write how a thing will turn up in the type—appear—take form.

July 25, 1889

I still have the instinct, the grasp, the pith, of the printer. It is like swimming—the stroke comes back however long and many the years since may have been.

July 23, 1888

I am sensitive to technical slips, errors—am as ready as anyone to have everything shipshape, or as nearly so as I can make them. I abhor slouchy workmen—always admonish them in offices doing my work: Don't put on a slouchy printer.

September 1, 1888

Why in the world do the printers—like the tailors—always pursue their own way, regardless of what others want or of what is best?

August 29, 1889

. . . he is to produce an Emerson—an early Emerson on which the copyright has expired. What a cute—devilishly cute—lot the publishing wolves are. There they are, the whole hungry herd—a dozen sets of eyes straining for a chance to pounce on these things the first minute of freedom.

August 21, 1888

Authors always growl about publishers, probably with a good deal of reason, too: but I don't know as the publisher is any different from the shirtman or the shoemaker or anybody else with goods to sell. All the little inhuman trickeries current are referred back to business.

May 17, 1888

I wonder that America—as would seem so natural, so fittingly the case—does not raise a race of publishers the finest, the broadest, the world has so far seen—publishers typical of our life here. Instead of having done this so far —instead of having raised one such man—we have had to

Whitman. Photograph by Phillips and Taylor, Philadelphia, about 1873. Autographed. Charles E. Feinberg Collection

get along with the most miserable, mean, tricky, circumscribed, hedged-in specimens the world has known—specimens I doubt if the outside world can parallel.

July 6, 1889

RADICAL & RADICALS

W. jumped on me for my "radical violence." "Some of your vehemence is all right—will stand: some of it is the impatience of youth. You must be on your guard—don't let your dislike for the conventions lead you to do the old things any injustice: lots of the old stuff is just as new as it is old. There is no doubt more than most of us see even in the stagnant pool. Be radical—be radical—be not too damned radical."

May 28, 1888

I am in favor of agitation—agitation—agitation and agitation: without the questioner, the agitator, the disturber, to hit away at our complacency, we'd get into a pretty pass indeed.

April 12, 1889

You radical young fellows don't see it as I do—don't quite so plainly comprehend, concede, that it is best for any man to be tried by fire, to draw all the shot of the reactionaries, the wise conservatives and the fool conservatives, the asses in authority, the granitic stupidities of the average world. It all has its place—all. I, too, used to grow impatient, angry, about it, but now I want it all to be spoken, heard, passed upon: I want the full fire of the enemy. If the work we try to do cannot stand up against the total opposition we may be sure we have gone off on a false scent.

July 8, 1888

Everybody comes here demanding endorsements: endorse this, endorse that: each man thinks I am radical his way: I suppose I am radical his way, but I am not radical his way alone.

April 25, 1888

I am radical of radicals—but I don't belong to any school: after I got done with it there wouldn't be much wealth left in private hands—that is, if my say was final.

May 27, 1888

I am as radical now as ever—just as radical—but I am not asleep to the fact that among radicals as among the others there are hoggishnesses, narrownesses, inhumanities, which at times almost scare me for the future—for the future belongs to the radical and I want to see him do good things with it.

April 9, 1888

. . . while the conventionals, on their side, are generally too timid, we, the radicals of us, on our side, are often too cocky.

August 13, 1888

Did you ever notice . . . that the bitterest, most severe, most malignant, conservatives—old conservatives—are made out of men who in their youth were the extremest radicals—radicals of radicals?

August 9, 1888

Although my philosophy includes conservatives, everything else being equal I prefer the radicals as men and companions.

October 4, 1888

....

RANK & FILE

....

8 P.M. . . . W. particularly interested as always in the state of things outdoors. . . . Gets great pleasure out of my recital of average experiences—particularly street incidents: likes me to tell him about people I meet—particularly everyday people. . . . I showed him . . . a review of November Boughs. W. read it while I stood looking over his shoulder. "It is kindly," he said—"very kindly: and that is much. . . ."

He put his name on a copy of the title page medallion. "Give it to Acton," he said. Acton is Bilstein's proofreader. . . . W. said: "Give him that: give him that for me. . . . I have a great emotional respect for the background people—for the folks who are not generally in-

cluded—for the absentees, the forgotten: the shy nobodies
who in the end are best of all."

November 2, 1888

··················

We can't get on with a world of masters: we want men
—a world of men: backbone men—the workers, the doers,
the humbles: we want them. The ornamental classes make
a lot of noise but they create nothing: you may crack a
whip over men and you may be useless nevertheless: lots in
business that passes for ability is only brutality: don't forget that—you masters: you are not so damned clever as
you think: you're only coarse, cruel, wanton: that's all:
that's all.

January 8, 1889

. . . the best plain men are always the best men, anyhow—if there is any better or best among men at all. The
cultivated people, the well-mannered people, the well-
dressed people, such people always seem a trifle overdone—
spoiled in the finish.

April 26, 1888

There were three classes who served nobly during the
[Civil] War to whom justice has never been done—the
telegraph boys, the cadet physicians, the nurses in the hospitals. Some day somebody will write all that down circum-
stantially. The trouble is that it looks now as if the thing
would be delayed till all the actors are dead. The telegraph
boys were a remarkable body: picked up here and there—
often waifs, mechanics, sometimes boys of well-to-do fami-
lies: they were wonderfully sharp-witted—distinguished so,
as a body: alert, active, bright, noble, industrious, temper-
ate. . . . There were clusters of them—clusters of clusters

of them: every general with some, every high officer with many: they did most valiant service: yet no one has ever raised a voice for them: oh! if I had but the power to do it! I wasted many of my own opportunities.

February 6, 7, 1889

It always struck me in the War, how honest and direct the private soldiers were—how superior they were, in the main, to their officers. They would freely unbosom to me— tell me of their experiences—perhaps go into minutest details—always, however, as if everything was a matter of fact, was of no value—as if nothing was of enough significance to be bragged of. Their stories justified themselves— did not need to be argued about.

August 14, 1888

It seems to me that of all modern men the transportation men most nearly parallel the ancients in ease, poise, simplicity, average nature, robust instinct, firsthandedness: are next the very a b c of real life.

February 1, 1889

I think there is no more important, valuable, necessary, class of men than the men who are under all conditions, all shifts of weather, all play of incident, unbaffled, undeviating, irrevocable.

February 7, 1889

. . . letter-carriers always seem a picked class—always seem of the best sort—only the best seem to gravitate to that business.

July 22, 1889

And what a tribe the tribe of the proofreaders is! I think some men, some writers, owe a great part of their reputations to the excellence of their proofreaders—to their vigilance, their counsel. Who can do justice to the cute, keen intellects of men of this stamp—their considerate patience, far-seeingness? Little credit is done them: they are snubbed, quibbled over, made light of: for twenty years I have had it more or less in mind to say my say—tell what I know—about the proofreaders: it is a debt I should long ago have paid.

April 5, 1889

It seems to be taken as one of the inalienable prerogatives of some of the best mechanics to get drunk: you know how true this is of the printers: often of the very best of them: then there are the hatters: they too I am told are tremendously addicted to the cup: there must be something in these confining occupations which induces thirst.

February 18, 1889

READING

7:45, evening. W. reading Memoirs of Bewick. "It is autobiographical," said W: "simple, plain, interesting." "Are you particularly interested in artists? You read a lot about Blake, Millet—." He replied: "I suppose I am, but not necessarily. The book just accidentally turned up—I have had it for years: so I tackle it again. . . . My reading is wholly without plan: the first thing at hand, that is the thing I take up."

October 17, 1888

■■■■■■■■■■■■■■■■■

I am not a constitutional reader: I do not apply myself to reading in the usual way. I have read, to be sure—read a good deal since I have been tied up indoors—but after all that has never been the chief thing with me.

May 20, 1888

I read by fits and starts—fragments: read in moods: no sequence, no order, no nothing.

October 17, 1888

I don't know but in reading the best method is to simply let the mind caper about and do as it chooses—or as it don't choose, as it must. I never try to create interest for myself in a book: if the interest don't come of its own account I drop my experiment: I would no more force my reading than my writing.

August 11, 1888

I will only come at an opinion of the book by waiting —very patient waiting. I read a book in which I have a special interest three times or more—once to get its capital features—then after some delay I go at it again—this time for its atmosphere, spirit, and so on: that's reading number two, remember: then comes number three: I read finally for conclusions.

May 16, 1888

I used to thrust papers, things, into my pockets: always had a lot of reading matter about my person somewhere: on ferries, cars, anywhere, I would read, read, read: it's a good habit to get into: have you ever noticed how most people absolutely waste most all their spare time?

April 6, 1889

RECOLLECTIONS

[Tuesday] W. in good shape. Speaks optimistically about his health. . . .

Back of him on the wall was a pencilled figure of a rather ragged looking nondescript. "Where did you get that?" I asked. "Would you believe it—the tramp himself was here this morning. He was a curious character—an itinerant poet: and he read me some of his poems: Lord pass him, what stuff! But it was his own, written on the road. It made me feel bad to think that he could go along in the sun and rain and write while I am housed up here in the dust of a dead room eking out my substance in coalstove words." "Coalstove" was good. But he burns wood in his stove. . . . He reflected as I left: "When I said goodbye to the tramp I was envious: I could not see what right he had to his monopoly of the fresh air. He said he was bound for some place in Maryland. I shall dream of Maryland tonight— dream of farm fences, barns, singing birds, sounds, all sorts, over the hills."

[Wednesday] W. not so well. "I am not down in the mouth about it," he explained, "but I am still jealous of that tramp: I suppose he's bummin' along somewhere on the road eatin' apples and feelin' drowsy and doin' as he pleases—and here am I in this room growlin' with a belly-ache.". . .

[Thursday] "I feel so good again today," W. assures me, "that I no longer envy the tramp. I think that dusty cuss did me lots of good. . . . I thought he had taken everything he had brought away with him again: but I was mistaken. He shook some of his dust off on me: that dust has taken effect."

April 3, 4, 5, 1888

....

. . . all ways are good if they are good ways—if they pan out well. I remember I used to have an intense dislike for eating in theatres—in such public places—seeing people eat—eating myself—especially women eating: but one evening I went into a theatre—it was hot and close—with a friend—and in the course of the play he nudged me: "Look there!" he said: and I looked: I found him pointing out a woman in front of us sucking an orange—violating my tradition: but doing it so inimitably—being no doubt warm and thirsty—doing it with such calm grace, cleanliness, I could not but admit that it justified itself. It is a good, the only, principle, to apply to art.

June 28, 1888

I never knew a typical deacon who was not in many respects lacking in the things we have a right to expect of a man. Generally, his standard is low. My first experience with that sort of a character was an unfortunate one: it has become a mere memory now, it was so long ago—but the impression it left upon me was ineradicable. The man I mean was a type—the very sort of a man I think I of all men doubt: a pious, sanctimonious, unctuous, oily individual: his victim was my father. I was a boy then—hardly more than ten years old if that old. A Methodist elder—don't the Methodists call them elders?—or something or other of that sort—contracted with my father, who was a builder, for the construction of a house—drawing up the contract so cutely from his own side—so shrewdly worded —as to make it possible for him, when the time for settlement came, to evade here a sum, there a sum, until my poor straightforward father was nearly swindled out of his boots. It was a sample case—I could match it with many incidents that have come my way since. I thoroughly disapprove of—hate—yes, even fear, institutional, official, teleological, goodness. I would any time rather trust myself in the hands of an avowed secular merchant. He is less likely to do you up.

June 3, 1888

I could tell you of a wonderful experience. . . . It was in Washington, during the war, in one of the wards of a hospital—a poor room with cheaper furniture than this you see in my parlor, which is poor enough: a three legged stool for an altarpiece—no light but the light of a candle: then a priest came and administered the sacrament to a poor soldier. The room was spare, blank—no furnishings: the hearers in the other beds seemed altogether incredulous or else altogether convinced: there was a suspicion of quackery, humbuggery, in the whole performance: no one among the observers except myself perhaps was respectful. I stood aside and watched, aroused in places to sympathy, though mainly impressed by the spectacular features of the event—

Whitman about 61 years old. Photograph by Gutekunst, Philadelphia.
The Historical Society of Pennsylvania

by its human emotional features. All was done solemnly, without noise—done in a way to appeal to your sense of right weight and measure—proportion, proportion.

May 12, 1888

. . . some of my best friends in the hospitals were probably Southern boys. I remember one in particular, right off—a Kentucky youngster (a mere youngster), illiterate, extremely: I wrote several letters for him to his parents: fine, honest, ardent, chivalrous. I found myself loving him like a son: he used to kiss me good night—kiss me. He got well, he passed out with the crowd, went home, the war was over. We never met again.

May 13, 1888

I remember another scene—a regiment, once made up of a thousand or twelve hundred men, returned from the war —from the battles, sieges, skirmishings, halts, marches, goings on—coming into Washington, perhaps on an errand only, for provisioning—God knows what: only there on duty for a day or more: now reduced from its proud twelve hundred to its humble one or two hundred men, trailing in, as it may be said, what remained of them, with their colors in rags and their faces emaciated, worn, but with their hearts true. Don't that beat a cathedral picture? I think it does—God! it does, it does! It makes your heart bleed. Then you worship—get down on your real knees.

May 12, 1888

. . . there in Brooklyn: we were coming down what was called Washington Hill together . . . one of the many walks I delighted to take with my dear, dear mother. I can

see it all, all, even now: the two of us there, the man ap-
proaching—my mother's voice: her hand as it was laid on
my arm. . . . The fellow came up—asked me for ten
cents: he had not eaten, &c. I growled out: "I'll give you
nothing": turned away. The man was drunk then: was evidently now far along in a week of dissipation—perhaps trying to get rid of the effects of it: anyway, in bad condition.
I was certain the ten cents more would but go . . . for
drink. We passed on. My mother spoke to me: she said
(laid her hand on my arm): "I know what you are thinking—I know you feel it would only add to his misery to
give him ten cents more now: I know about such men: when
they get into that state then nothing can be done for the
moment but give them the drink: it is but mercy to give
it to them.". . . She was quiet, tender: I looked at her as
if to ask, What? she continuing: "I wish you had given
him the money: I would have you go back and give it to
him yet." So I went back, complied—we resumed our walk.
January 3, 1889

Thoreau had his own odd ways. Once he got to the
house while I was out—went straight to the kitchen where
my dear mother was baking some cakes—took the cakes
hot from the oven. He was always doing things of the
plain sort—without fuss. I liked all that about him. But
Thoreau's great fault was disdain—disdain for men (for
Tom, Dick and Harry): inability to appreciate the average life—even the exceptional life: it seemed to me a
want of imagination. He couldn't put his life into any other
life—realize why one man was so and another man was
not so: was impatient with other people on the street and so
forth. We had a hot discussion about it—it was a bitter
difference: it was rather a surprise to me to meet in Thoreau such a very aggravated case of superciliousness. It was

egotistic—not taking that word in its worst sense. . . . We could not agree at all in our estimate of men—of the men we meet here, there, everywhere—the concrete man. Thoreau had an abstraction about man—a right abstraction: there we agreed. We had our quarrel only on this ground. Yet he was a man you would have to like—an interesting man, simple, conclusive. . . . I asked Sanborn *
. . . who of all men of Concord was most likely to last into the future. Sanborn took his time in replying. I thought he was going to say Emerson, but he didn't. He said Thoreau. I was surprised—looked at him—asked: "Is that your deliberate judgment?" and he said very emphatically: "Yes!" I thought that very significant. Considering who Emerson was, Thoreau was, Sanborn was, very, very significant.

May 26, 1888

•••

RELIGION

•••

Improvement in W.'s condition today. He seems to alternate bad with good days. . . . In his mail was a postal card from Paris addressed to him as "the American poet." This is what was written on the card:

"Read the histories of Lourdes and LaSalette, and, if

---

* Franklin Benjamin Sanborn (1831–1917), Concord, Massachusetts schoolteacher, abolitionist, and author of books about Thoreau, Alcott, Emerson, and Hawthorne. W. T.

you relish them, the lives of St. Peter and Paul (Catholic).
You might also read the *Catholic* life of Jesus Christ. Pray
Sts. Peter and Paul to cure you and have votive masses (P.
and P.) prayers and communions made on 29 June, 30
June and 1 August. Buy pictures of them and hang them
in your room; or buy statues. P. and P. will be pleased at
your intercession."

This was unsigned. W. remarked: "When I was in Washington it was surprising how many Catholic priests I came
to know—how many took the trouble to get acquainted
with me—on what good terms we kept with each other. I
think we were unified on the strength of the deeply religious, deeply adoring, spirit that was patent behind our differences of technology, theology—our differences of lingo,
name. Perhaps this postal is the reflection of that experience
—grew out of it—who knows? I do not make light of such
messages—indeed, they have a profound place in my consideration. Of course I haven't a particle of faith in
Lourdes—in faith cures—bones of saints, such things—not a
shred of it—not the first sign of a sign of it—but this postal
has for me a meaning quite apart from the literal yes or no
of Lourdes—a meaning at least of sympathy, helpfulness,
service. People often speak of the Leaves as wanting in religion, but that is not my view of the book—and I ought
to know. I think the Leaves the most religious book among
books: crammed full of faith. What would the Leaves be
without faith? An empty vessel: faith is its very substance,
balance—its one article of assent—its one item of assurance."

June 23, 1888

....

I claim everything for religion: after the claims of my
religion are satisfied nothing is left for anything else: yet I

have been called irreligious—an infidel (God help me!) : as if I could have written a word of the Leaves without its religious root-ground. I am not traditionally religious—I know it: but even traditionally I am not anti: I take all the old forms and faiths and remake them in conformity with the modern spirit, not rejecting a single item of the earlier programs.

April 2, 1888

. . . every man has a religion: has something in heaven or earth which he will give up everything else for—something which absorbs him, possesses itself of him, makes him over into its image: something: it may be something regarded by others as being very paltry, inadequate, useless: yet it is his dream, it is his lodestar, it is his master. That, whatever it is, seized upon me, made me its servant, slave: induced me to set aside the other ambitions: a trail of glory in the heavens, which I followed, followed, with a full heart. When once I am convinced I never let go: I had to pay much for what I got but what I got made what I paid for it much as it was seem cheap. I had to give up health for it—my body—the vitality of my physical self: oh! much had to go—much that was inestimable, that no man should give up until there is no longer any help for it . . . and what did I get for it? I never weighed what I gave for what I got but I am satisfied with what I got.

January 20, 1889

I get very impatient some days—am a little resentful: sore, sore: wonder if it's all fair and square—whether the scheme after all is not doubtful: then I go back: find my way back to my central thought again—my spinal conviction: I resent my resentment—am ashamed of my questions. I feel

how empty everything would seem if I was not full of this
faith—if this faith did not overflow me: how useless all
things would be if they led on to nothing but what we see—
to nothing but what we appear to wind up in here.

December 16, 1888

. . . it is best we should not know too definitely what is
to come: the important thing to us now is the life here—
the people here: yes, that's the important immediate thing:
the earth struggle—our effort, our task, here to build up
our human social body into finer results: the daily hourly
job right here, right now: yours, mine: the rest will come
—the beyond: we are not called upon to bother about it at
once: it would only confuse matters: we can make our
declaration about it, say our yes, then stop: our responsi-
bilities are on the earth.

December 16, 1888

I believe in immortality, and by that I mean *identity*. I
know I have arrived at this result more by what may be
called feeling than formal reason—but I believe it: yes, I
know it.

May 6, 1888

Mystery is not the denial of reason but its honest con-
firmation: reason, indeed, leads inevitably to mystery—but,
as you know, mystery is not superstition: mystery and
reality are the two halves of the same sphere.

July 14, 1888

There's a spiritual side of the simplest physical phenomena: not only a spiritual side: more than that: a spiritual outcome.

January 25, 1889

I believe in saints if they're far enough off.

May 6, 1888

. . . asceticism is always obscene to me.

December 19, 1888

The whole miracle dogma business has been swung as a club over the head of the world: it has been a weapon flourished by the tyrannical dynasties of the old world—dynasties murderous, reeking, unscrupulous, barbarous: they have always tried to justify their crimes by an assumed divine grant of some sort. I have often wondered about the Greeks—how much of their mythology they really believed: it looks to me as if their gods like other gods were mostly used not for liberation but oppression: the gods intervened, but often in mean, despicable, poisonous, dastardly ways.

March 15, 1889

After you have got rid of all your dogmas then you can read the Bible—realize its immensity—not till then.

July 12, 1888

. . . when I was a young fellow up on the Long Island shore I seriously debated whether I was not by spiritual bent a Quaker?—whether if not one I should become one?

But the question went its way again: I put it aside as impossible: I was never made to live inside a fence.

July 19, 1888

I anticipate the day when some wise man will start out to argue that two and two are not four but five or something else: history proving that two and two couldn't be four: and probability, too: yes, more than that, the wise man will prove it out of his own consciousness—prove it for somebody—for a few: they will believe in him—a body of disciples will believe: then, presto! you have a new religion!

September 15, 1888

THE SCIENTIFIC SPIRIT

1.40 P.M. W. reading. Looked well. First time in several weeks that I've seen him by daylight. "Tom was in—came an hour or so ago—and your sister, too: Mrs. Harned. I was so glad she came up. It has been nine months since I have seen her: a long spell for her as well as for me." Then he paused a minute. "Yes: there were other visitors, too: Billings, or somebody: he came with a couple of young fellows." I asked: "You mean Bilstein?" he responding: "Yes, yes: simply one of the in and out visits: we talked a little bit about printing—plate printing: he appeared to be an adept—know his business. I liked him; liked 'em all: he was very quiet: I get on so well with plain people." . . .

W. wanted to know whether the river was frozen across. He said: "I once hobbled about half way over with my cane: the ice got unreliable then: I had to turn back." Said of Burroughs: "John is not so wonderful about people as about bugs: he sees some things with wonderful clarity of comprehension: there are other things which he sees rather dimly. My feeling about people, about the universe, becomes more and more superphysical—is more and more emphatic in its mystical intimations. In reading John of late I have felt that his studies were drawing him the other way. Perhaps I'm getting mixed: I may not interpret him fairly: so I do not offer my impression as final. It always amazes me when a man of science drifts off into materialism: I look to every man of science to maintain the assertion of omnipresent unmitigated never terminable life: when he does anything else I suspect him of being false to his standards of truth. This may sound like inexcusable dogmatism, though I offer it in any but a dogmatic spirit."

February 3, 1889

....

I have great faith in science—real science: the science that is the science of the soul as well as the science of the body (you know many men of half sciences seem to forget the soul).

August 4, 1888

I like the scientific spirit—the holding off, the being sure but not too sure, the willingness to surrender ideas when the evidence is against them: this is ultimately fine—it always keeps the way beyond open—always gives life, thought, affection, the whole man, a chance to try over again after a mistake—after a wrong guess.

May 4, 1888

. . . the crowning characteristic, the final glory, of our age is in this—that it is an age of inquiry: inquiry that enters everything—everything sacred or profane: with no spot anywhere but someone wants to explore it. I know every age is in some measure an age of inquiry, but I don't think there ever was an age that so daringly, so persistently, everywhere, insisted upon its right to investigate.

April 3, 1889

....

SEX

....

8 P.M. W. up to his recent best standard today. Visitors few. . . .

W. asked me about my sister. . . . He said: "She went through that business of having a baby like the sun comes up in the morning . . . . We have got so in our civilization, so-called (which is no civilization at all) that we are afraid to face the body and its issues—when we shrink from the realities of our bodily life: when we refer the functions of the man and the woman, their sex, their passion, their normal necessary desires, to something which is to be kept in the dark and lied about instead of being avowed and gloried in. . . . though we will not allow it to be freely spoken of [it] is still the basis of all that makes life worth while and advances the horizon of discovery. Sex: sex: sex: whether you sing or make a machine, or go to the North Pole, or love your mother, or build a house, or black shoes, or anything —anything at all—it's sex, sex, sex: sex is the root of it all: sex—the coming together of men and women: sex, sex."

He stopped at this point. I cried: "I wish you had kept on, Walt!" He said: "Why should I? I have got it all said: sex, sex: always immanent: here with us discredited—not suffered: rejected from our art: yet still sex, sex: the root of roots: the life below the life!"

January 3, 1889

SICKNESS

W. is always saying to me—"I am nearly blind." He does have trouble with his eyes. But he sees things, too. Tonight he said: "One of the worst signs is my eyes—they seem to be going back on me entirely—I can't see an elephant with 'em." Right afterwards while I was looking at a photograph of the Symonds home at Davos Platz sent him by Symonds W. remarked: "And do you notice Symonds himself is down there by the shed, large as life?" I did notice Symonds. But he wasn't large as life. He was so small it would take divination or a magnifier to see him. I said so to W. and added, rallying him: "And you are the man who says he is blind!"

To which W. testily replied: "Who should so well know he is blind as the man who can't see!" I laughed and was about to ask him another question but he would not let me. "Take your questions to court—don't bother me with them: you ought to be a detective or a lawyer!"

June 8, 1888

....

I am all right—good for the night: let him [the nurse] come back in the morning. I would rather be alone. I hate to have anybody around, right in my room, watching me.

June 10, 1888

The worst of sickness is its bad humor, its peevishness, its crossness, its irritability.

September 4, 1888

It is hard for a perfectly well man to thoroughly understand a perfectly sick man, or vice versa.

August 31, 1888

When you argue about health your health is already gone.

August 24, 1888

A great big lubber like me (my burly body—red, full face)—gets very little credit for being sick—for being an invalid.

June 5, 1888

In physical peculiarity I seem to be both fathered and mothered—both of my parents may be seen in me. I attribute much of my success in weathering this attack to my good stock—to my father, my mother: indeed, not one mother alone—the mothers of five or six generations.

June 19, 1888

I find my digestive apparatus still fitful—still unwilling to do its work smoothly. First it fires up—raises hell—then it gets down so low we have to bust our lungs blowing it into flame again.

June 14, 1888

I do poorly, poorly: this has been as bad a day as any since my sickness began. I do not suffer pain—only great feebleness, inertness, incapacity to think, to see—yes, a sort of general debility of the system. I am convinced that I am in a baddish state—that I have received a severe shock which is not easily, maybe not at all, to be shaken off. But I still hope on—I do not give up: expect a clear day yet. . . . I have eaten my meals today with some relish—so the trouble don't seem to be primarily with my heart or my stomach. I do not seem to want to go downstairs or out of doors—that is the worst sign of all: I alternate between my bed and chair all day long.

June 20, 1888

I don't seem to be a hospital person: I rebel against the idea of being nursed, cared for: but it's of no avail: here I am, tied up to the wharf, rotting in the sun.

February 2, 1889

I have thought something very interesting, valuable, suggestive, might be written about the influence, good influence, bad influence, of sickness (disease) in literature. Another

Whitman. Photograph by Cox, about 1887. Autographed. Charles E. Feinberg Collection

thing: the influence of drink in literature . . . would also be instructive: it has so many sides, noble, devilish: it would need to be rightly interpreted—not by a puritan, not by a toper (the puritan is only another kind of toper).

May 13, 1888

I am getting to be a sort of monologuer: it is a disease that grows on a man who has no legs to walk on.

October 9, 1888

I am subject to a new development of my trouble—a new phase—seen the last few days—what it is I do not know . . . a strange, soggy, wet, sticky ineligibility as of tar, falling down over me each morning for three or four hours, putting me into a state of almost death-like impotency— though I am always aware of things all the time just the same.

June 22, 1888

Navigation grows increasingly difficult. It now takes all my energy merely to get to the chair and back to the bed again. I am not hopeless, however: I am a good wrestler.

July 19, 1888

See—I am off again—talking about my health—as if there was nothing in the world but my pains and aches to be considered.

July 6, 1888

The worst thing with an old man when he is sick is that he sees nothing ahead—that for him, is nothing but reverse, down-hill. A young fellow, when he is sick—when he is poor

—when he is troubled—has everything before him, but a man old, quite old, who has been badly whacked, as I have, has but to wait and expect an end.

July 23, 1889

··

SMOKING, EATING & DRINKING

··

7.30 P.M. W. reading the paper. Was cheerful. Ready to talk. "The good spell," he said, "still persists." . . .

W. talked of his Washington life. "William [O'Connor] was truly a temperance man: in the real sense so: he used to enjoy wine—an occasional glass, as I do, but no more." Did O'C smoke? "No: nor do I—nor did I ever: and John [Burroughs] the same: we were a no-smoking crowd." I said: "You don't object when the smokers who come here commiserate with you over what you have lost by not smoking. You keep still. You don't have any regrets in the matter, do you?" "Not one regret: only satisfaction: sometime there will be a change: now most men smoke—then most men will not smoke: the tobacco habit may have its joys but it also has other integers that are neither glad nor beautiful: it's one of the avenues through which people today get rid of some of their nerve surplus: it goes with things as they are: but it is so filthy a practice taken for all in all that I can't see but people must inevitably grow away from it."

January 29, 1889

·················

You can't make rules of diet or rules of anything else to suit everybody. I am more likely to have feelings than theories about things: I was never a man to drive doctrines to death—to take up with fads, special providences, whims of diet or manners.

October 11, 1888

I think my diet needs some careful revision, though I am not a reckless eater any time. We can—if we learn how—regulate diet for ourselves but can regulate it for no second person: one man's taste may be as different—is sure to be—from another's as meat is different from a potato.

June 13, 1888

It's a strong weak diet . . . I mean that it is strong of its kind but a damn weak kind.

February 4, 1889

There seem to be swigs and swigs—swigs that do the business and swigs that do not.

March 16, 1889

The great thing with me is the *spirit:* as the old man said, my *spirit is tremenjuous—tremenjuous,* thanks to myself in part, thanks in part to an occasional sip of sherry.

May 17, 1889

. . . if I had the means of doing so here I should break a bottle of champagne every day. It does me no harm.

May 25, 1889

....

THE SOCIAL ORDER

....

Harned brought some pears. Then talked with W. about politics. W. spoke with great force. . . . "The great country, the greatest country, the richest country, is not that which has the most capitalists, monopolists, immense grabbings, vast fortunes, with its sad, sad foil of extreme, degrading, damning poverty, but the land in which there are the most homesteads, freeholds—where wealth does not show such contrasts high and low, where all men have enough—a modest living—and no man is made possessor beyond the sane and beautiful necessities of the simple body and the simple soul. The great country, in fact, is the country of free labor—of free laborers: negro, white, Chinese, or other. To use the word 'great' to describe any other sort of country is to my mind a confession of ignorance or hypocrisy. I do not mean this to be counted as an expression of despair: men are in the main decent, pure, or want to be. Things are about as good as they can be under present conditions (of course man can always change the conditions). Systems, institutions, even the vile ones, have a work to do —do the work." Harned asked: "What place do you find for corruption in politics?" W. answered: "I do not need to find a place for it: it has found a place for itself. But there's more to the story than that, Tom—oh! much more. The spiritual influences back of everything else—subtle, unseen, invisible, mainly discredited—they finally arbitrate the social order. Science tells us about the excretions—the throwings off of the body—that the chief results are secured in the form of invisible exhalations—the whole flesh casting it forth. That strange, inarticulate, force is not less operative in the institutions of society—in politics, literature, music, science, art—than in the physical realm. We must not forget such forces—not one of them. Society throws off some of its ephemera, its corruption, through politics—the process is offensive—we shudder over it—but it may be true, it is still true, that the interior system throwing off its excreta this way is sound, wholly sound, prepared for the proper work of its own purification."

August 3, 1888

••••••••••••••••••

I don't care which sea the ship comes on so it finally gets home—I don't care who brings the wheat or by what route it is brought so the wheat is good to the man who brings and the man who receives it.

August 2, 1888

. . . people get accustomed to a certain order of traditions, forms: they think these a part of nature, or nature itself—that they are never to be displaced, are eternal: they will not be easily shaken out of their conviction even when they know all their vitality has departed.

March 16, 1889

. . . there are times when the house cannot be patched any more but *asks to be taken down.*

March 16, 1889

. . . things drive us on—the God damned robbers, fools, stupids, who ride their gay horses over the bodies of the crowd: they drive us on: God knows to what: sometimes I don't like to think of it: but they'll drive us into an inevitable resentment, then revolt, of some sort. The prospect of it all would make me shudder if I didn't know that something must happen—that we can't push on much farther in this direction.

December 30, 1888

Society would go to pieces if its guardians didn't protect it against the inroads of rebellion.

October 25, 1888

In the South they have what they call a chivalry: a toplofticality: it is not a real chivalry—not by a damn sight: what men may call the moral toplofticality that belongs to the North: here is a distinct difference: they are behind the North, anyone can see it—behind it at least a generation. They will evolve—but will they ever catch up?

March 12, 1889

I for my part am distrustful of any personal rules of public customs which interpose barriers between the leaders and the people. I like all fraternization between leaders, people, the masses: no travesty of reserve.

October 30, 1888

. . . one half: oh! three quarters, of the sociology of America consists in keeping genteel.

September 12, 1888

I think our people are getting entirely too decent. They like nice white hands, men and women. They are too much disturbed by dirt. They need the open air, coarse work—physical tasks: something to do away from the washstand and the bathtub. God knows, I'm not opposed to clean hands. But clean hands, too, may be a disgrace.

April 22, 1888

[The] whole serving business is a stench: it is offensive to me: besides, I believe people who serve you without love get even behind your back.

May 18, 1888

The Greeks . . . the writers, the race traditions: are full of this idea: the idea that the gods hate prosperity—this sort of prosperity: the idea that when men sit heaped all around with possessions, loot, then the end is near—then look out.

November 12, 1888

. . . money never made any man free—only enslaves men . . .

January 8, 1889

Yes—many's the thing liberty has got to do before we have achieved liberty!

November 9, 1888

....

TEMPO

....

Dropt in at W.'s early morning. All well. W. asleep. W.
on his bed in the evening when I arrived—7.45. Stayed until
9.30. He was very communicative. I put in few questions.
Yet he talked on. No light—day gradually going; we sat by
and bye in total darkness. . . . Excused himself for his
inability to attack the proofs. "There they are, untouched
—God help me!" . . . Discussed hurry. W. aware of the
situation. "If I can't get at it for good tomorrow I'll resign
the whole business into your hands." Added: "Hurry was
never another name for Walt Whitman."

June 18, 1888

....

There may be reasons for hurrying but I can't hurry anyway: I'm no hurrier: I couldn't hurry if the house was on
fire.

February 21, 1889

I am a very slow worker—I take my work easy—but
when I get going I am quite steady and accomplish a good
deal.

May 20, 1888

My mind is a slow one—it never hustles . . .

August 6, 1888

I had, I may say, an unusual capacity for standing still, rooted on a spot, at a rest, for a long spell, to ruminate— hours in and out sometimes.

July 25, 1888

I must have a thing by me a long while—must give it a chance to sink in—things never come fast with me, though, to be sure, when they come they come firm. That is why I would not make a good journalist, preacher—least of all a doctor. My opinions are all, always, so hazy—so slow to come. I am no use in any situation which calls for instant decision.

June 2, 1888

. . . I boil: burn up: but often I keep my mouth shut: I am a slow mover: I don't hurry even in my tantrums: my passions are all ready for action but—well, there are many buts.

January 26, 1889

. . . all things, go so slow with me . . . everything in me proceeds by degrees—a sort of calm steady undeviating procrastination: things which come to a head in some people at once require time in me.

February 5, 1889

I am more famous for procrastination than for anything else: you write to him—tell him that Walt Whitman will be along by and bye—is rather lame in the legs and in several other things : is harder to move round than a sick elephant.

May 13, 1888

The surgeons there in the hospitals got onto my trouble before I did myself. I seem to be remarkably constituted in one way—for being slow to affect things or be affected. I would never take a disease in a hurry—never make a convert in a hurry—and so on, so on. The trouble at Washington was the culmination of an unusual sympathetic and emotional expenditure of vital energy during those years [18]63–4–5 : partly this and perhaps directly from the singular humor of a New York lad there in the hospitals who demanded to have me—would accept no one but me— to see him through his trouble—a whim quite frequently encountered in sick people. I attended to him—bound his wounds—did everything possible for him. He was an extreme case—an awful case—dangerous at any time as a charge. The effect upon me was slow, though one of the surgeons there finally called my attention to my own peril. He said that what would have made itself manifest in most others at once took a long time to appear in me. Even now, when they give me medicine, which in other men acts in an hour or two, it sometimes takes a day or two for that medicine to take effect. I always was deliberate—except for my vigor much as you see me now.

July 25, 1888

I am a slow arriver : I get there but I always come in last.

May 16, 1888

VARIETIES OF MAN

7.45 P.M. W. reading paper. . . . Has to shade his eyes as he reads. Stops often. . . .

The word "humor," he said, always "mystified" him. "I think Shakespeare had it—had it to the full: but there have been others—great men, too—who had little or none of it. The question is, was Shakespeare's humor good natured? Good nature is the important equation in humor. . . . They do charge me, as you say, with lacking humor: it never seemed to me it could be true: but I don't dispute it: I only see myself from the inside—with the ordinary prejudice a fellow has in favor of himself . . . . The idea that anybody imagines I can't appreciate a joke or even make jokes seems preposterous. Do you find me as infernally impossible as that, Horace? Bryant said to me in one of our chats: 'The most humorous men I have met have been the lightest laughers.' You can't always tell by a man's guffaws whether he is a real humorist or not."

January 22, 1889

There is in some men an indefinable something which flows out and over you like a flood of light—as if they possessed it illimitably—their whole being suffused with it.

May 2, 1889

. . . the indefinable attractiveness of some men: we cannot describe it any more than why we are attracted by a tree, a field, a boat, a road—only we know that it is and that is all.

October 18, 1888

Sometimes we see united in one man the very highest type of conscientiousness—the most exalted, superior, one may say perfect, moral sense—the largest consideration of the transcendental impetus to action—with an average capacity for taking care of everyday life, bank bills, farms, houses, stocks, and so forth.

July 9, 1888

I don't think there can be any great character, really great character, without centrality—some prevailing idea, some purpose at heart: more and more that conviction possesses me, absorbs me.

March 15, 1889

. . . genius is almost a hundred per cent directness—nothing more.

August 7, 1888

It is hard to make or justify comparisons of great men: stars differ in glory: who shall say one star is eminent beyond the rest of the stars? But we have an instinct in the matter—you have yours, I have mine. Shall we quarrel about the stars?

April 26, 1888

I like salient men—the men of elements—oxygenated men: the fellers who come and go like storms come and go: who grow up out of honest roots: not the titillated gentleman of boudoir amours and parlor fripperies: no, not that man: but if need be the rough of the streets who may underneath his coarse skin possess the saving graces of sympathy, service—the first of all, the last of all, the heart of all, personal excellence.

August 21, 1888

I have often been accused of undervaluing the leaders—of exaggerating the importance of the *miserable*—of unreasonably exalting the rank and file. Military men have often taken me up on that score—have said: "If you will look, you cannot but see that officers are as important as men." I might say "yes" to that: yet I see more than that, too.

October 23, 1888

We meet people—men, women—not intellectual, not literary, to whom we are drawn, who are drawn towards us: we do not know what draws us—could not tell why we are drawn: yet the fact is indisputable—the bond is unseverable. This quality, whatever it is, the intellectualists, as such, lack: they are as humans to be avoided. The world in our time seems full of intellectual people: full: you meet them everywhere: the professions particularly are overweighted with them: but literature suffers worst of all from their invasion: the mal-development there is the most marked—is there most repulsive, most painful.

February 23, 1889

Whitman. Photograph by Cox, about 1887. Whitman called it "The
Laughing Philosopher"

It is curious, what are people's likes and dislikes—how their hates appear and remain, as well as their loves. You will find one man who hates another worse than the devil, exhibiting almost a snake-like poisonous antipathy, and yet can give no reason for it, has no reason for it—simply knows he feels it, that is all.

August 5, 1888

. . . it may not be the wise thing to say any nation or any class is at the top—only that individuals are farthest forward, that it is purely an individual matter.

April 13, 1889

. . . I have had wonderful good luck anyhow in my life to have met a number of . . . originals—not men of usual build, of usual ways, but men inherently set apart, a world each for himself.

April 23, 1889

You mustn't think I object to odd views when they come natural to a man—are a part of a man. I only object to them when they are put on for effect.

August 1, 1888

I hope that is the keystone of the arch of my teachings—allowing a place for every man's personality, idiosyncracy.

June 16, 1889

We can never truly know a man till we have seen him in his habitat.

January 26, 1889

You can detect the bent of the editorial mind with perfect ease by what it quotes.

August 9, 1888

The objections to me are the objections made to all men who choose to go their own road—make their own choice of methods.

July 16, 1888

. . . his don't-care-a-damnativeness was sublime.

February 17, 1889

He is not the biggest man I know but his "hello" is just as sweet to me as any other "hello."

July 7, 1888

. . . he was only a fool: there was only a dim light in his noddle: he had to steer by that light: what else could he do?

January 6, 1889

Some men stay in the rear with the beef and beans . . .

August 1, 1888

That man is a Rip Van Winkle—not up to the time: is still hurrahing for King George!

July 13, 1888

There's a certain allowance of deviltry in all boys. The boys out in this street probably know there is a sore, nervous old man up in his room, so they fling their malignant rattle-snake poison about with special vehemence. Boys could not

get along without that. But let them go on—don't interfere
with them. It would worry me more to have that done than
to bear with the noise.

June 30, 1888

"Christian gentleman"! He is an unknown quantity, almost! There are few "Christian gentlemen"—in fact, we
do not know what a Christian gentleman is . . . the
"Christian gentleman" is a rare bird!—so rare he is never
found at all!

June 19, 1889

WAR

To W.'s at one o'clock. Sat in chair. Bright and chatty—
"garrulous," he said of himself. He had been rooting in
an old basket of odds and ends, "destroying a lot of stuff,
saving some"—looking at me with reassuring eyes: "I
haven't destroyed anything it was better to keep.". . .

He showed me several of his little improvised note-books
of the war-time. One was marked "September & October,
1863." He read some memoranda from it to me. "I carried
sometimes half a dozen such books in my pocket at one
time—never was without one of them: I took notes as I
went along—often as I sat—talking, maybe, as with you
here now—I writing while the other fellow told his story.

I would take the best paper (you can see, the best I could find) and make it up into these books, tying them with string or tape or getting someone (often it was Nellie O'Connor) to stitch them for me. My little books were be-ginnings—they were the ground into which I dropped the seed. . . . I would work in this way when I was out in the crowds, then put the stuff together at home. Drum Taps was all written in that manner—all of it—all put together by fits and starts, on the field, in the hospitals, as I worked with the soldier boys. . . . I want to give you one, several, of these books, if you would like to have them from me. They are more than precious—precious because they recall the old years—bring back the pictures of agony and death —reassociate me with the scenes and human actors of that tragic period."

August 14, 1888

....

I don't think the war seemed so horrible to me at the time, when I was busy in the midst of its barbarism, as it does now, in retrospect.

May 23, 1888

I never once have questioned the decision that led me into the War: whatever the years have brought—whatever sickness, what not—I have accepted the results as inevitable and right. This is the very centre, circumference, umbillicus, of my whole career.

November 14, 1888

I was in the midst of it all—saw war where war is worst —not on the battlefields, no—in the hospitals: there war is worst: there I mixed with it: and now I say God damn the wars—all wars: God damn every war: God damn 'em! God damn 'em! . . . I shouldn't let myself go—no, I shouldn't—but I say God damn 'em anyway!

December 13, 1888

O God! that whole damned war business is about nine hundred and ninety nine parts diarrhoea to one part glory: the people who like the wars should be compelled to fight the wars: they are hellish business, wars—all wars.

December 13, 1888

THE WAY OF THE WORLD

8.05 P.M. W. reading Lounsbery's [Thos. R. Lounsbury] "Cooper." Room mostly closed—rather warm. The day had been fine again. W. himself asked: "It has been another warm day, hasn't it?"—adding as to his own condition that it had only been so-so . . . .

Harned came in and was heartily greeted. W. inquired after Tom, after the family. . . . Harned said he had witnessed a base-ball match this afternoon. W. then asked: "Tell me, Tom—I want to ask you a question: in base-ball, is it the rule that the fellow who pitches the ball aims to pitch it in such a way the batter cannot hit it? Gives it a twist—what not—so it slides off, or won't be struck fairly?" And on Tom's affirmative—"Eh? that's the modern rule then, is it? I thought something of the kind—I read the papers about it—it seemed to indicate that there." Then he denounced the custom roundly. "The wolf, the snake, the cur, the sneak, all seem entered into the modern sportsman —though I ought not to say that, for the snake is snake because he is born so, and man the snake for other reasons, it may be said. . . . I should call it everything that is damnable."

May 7, 1889

On the whole the law is as likely to defraud you as to give you justice—quite as likely.

May 26, 1888

Little do judges and juries—especially judges—know about the truth: lots of men are just liars—remember that, too.

May 26, 1888

The world is so topsy turvy, so afraid to love, so afraid to demonstrate, so good, so respectable, so aloof, that when it sees two people or more people who really, greatly, wholly care for each other and say so—when they see such people they wonder and are incredulous or suspicious or defamatory, just as if they had somehow been the victims of an outrage. . . . For instance, any demonstration between men—any: it is always misjudged: people come to conclusions about it: they know nothing, there is nothing to be known; nothing except what might just as well be known: yet they shake their wise heads—they meet, gossip, generate slander: they know what is not to be known—they see what is not to be seen: so they confide in each other, tell the awful truth: the old women men, the old men women, the guessers, the false-witnesses—the whole caboodle of liars and fools.

December 25, 1888

. . . if there are 301 different ways of interpreting a passage—300 right, 1 wrong—the great mass will hit upon that wrong interpretation, insist upon it, dogmatize.

July 14, 1889

. . . when the world has it in for a man he does not have to do anything to furnish it with pretexts for vituperation, slander, persecution.

February 9, 1889

. . . the thing you don't wish circulated goes the rounds: it is copied from one end of the land to the other: the thing you wish noticed, read—think *must* be read beyond a doubt —that falls flat, is altogether forgotten.

January 11, 1889

We are not always patted on the back—sometime we are kicked on the behind: and who knows but the kicks do as much good as the pats.

June 2, 1888

It is always so: the tree with the best apples gets the worst clubbing.

May 9, 1888

. . . the world rarely seems except by and by to know its real inhabitants. The world goes daffy after phantom great men—the noisy epaulette sort: a man has got to set up a howl if he wants people to take him right off: if you have the real stuff in you you've got to wait for it to be recognized: and you are far more likely to die than to live in waiting.

January 18, 1889

The world insists on having its own way: it don't want a man so much the way he looks as the way it is accustomed to having men look.

May 14, 1888

. . . that is what they are all doing, all society, all professionalism, in books, poems, sermons—a strain to make an impression—everything loved that will dazzle the beholder, everything hated that will not.

August 2, 1888

I know everything in this world is a compromise—there is always an opposite word somewhere.

April 27, 1889

It is singular how people may get to believe they are saying a new thing when they are simply rehashing a very ancient text.

July 28, 1888

The world is turning around again towards the simple—the condition in which each man may supply his own needs.

A day may yet arrive to find us grown aboriginal again—
civilized aboriginal if I may say so.

August 17, 1888

I don't want the brotherhood of the world to be so long
a-coming. I can wait till it comes—it is sure to come—but
if I can hurry it by a day or so I am going to do so.

June 3, 1888

....

WOMEN

....

8 P.M. W. sitting by the light reading Symonds' Greek
Literature. . . . Fire rather low. W. took up a prodigious
log there by the stove: started to put it in: it would just
about go through the doorway. "There, Mr. Log," he said:
"I have been preserving you just for this moment: now
show what you can do!". . .

I put in this question: "You have said William [O'Con-
nor] was an Anarchist, too: how can he be both a party Republican and an Anarchist?" W. replied: "A Republican for
to-day, an Anarchist for to-morrow." He talked of O'Connor's tenure—his job: how he had been able to hold on to
it. "Even under Cleveland—radical as O'Connor is: and
[Sumner Increase] Kimball, too, his chief, just as radical
. . . ." I grouped W.'s Washington friends: called them
"the faithful few." W. said: "Yes, indeed: and there were
several more than you have ever heard of—the names for-

gotten now: Knox, one of them: a good, faithful fellow: and there was a musician, too: I used to run round and hear him play . . . . There were women, too: the women are wonderful friends: did you ever know one good noble genuine woman will outweigh all the rest? oh! I have been fortunate in these, too: fortunate! fortunate!"

January 19, 1889

····················

I have been more than lucky in the women I have met: a woman is always heaven or hell to a man—mostly heaven: she don't spend much of her time on the border-lines.

August 14, 1888

They say, somebody says, almost everybody says, there's a woman at the bottom of everything. That's the half truth: the whole truth is that there's a man always back of the woman.

August 27, 1888

I consider it the glory of this age that it dares throw off restrictions—throws them right and left: demands to go free: and this freedom must be for the women as well as the men. I look to see woman take her place in literature, in art—show what are her innate potencies, powers, attributes.

January 11, 1889

Leaves of Grass is essentially a woman's book: the women do not know it, but every now and then a woman shows that she knows it: it speaks out the necessities, its cry is the cry of the right and wrong of the woman sex—of the woman first of all, of the facts of creation first of all—of the feminine: speaks out loud: warns, encourages, persuades, points the way.

September 16, 1888

There's a beautiful woman: she is not beautiful alone or chiefly because of her eyes, her complexion, the mellowness of her body, though these, too, play their parts, but because of a certain unity, atmosphere, a certain balance of light and shade, which accounts for every detail—finally gives the detail its proper environment: yes, takes leave of the detail in the whole.

May 6, 1888

. . . our modern ideals of what constitutes a pretty face, —are damnable!

June 14, 1889

Our women don't seem to be any longer built for child-bearing. We have gone on for so long hurting the body that the job of rehabilitating it seems prodigious if not impossible.

August 16, 1888

I know of nothing more beautiful, inspiring, significant: a hale old woman, full of cheer as of years, who has raised a brood of hearty children, arriving at last at the period of rest, content, contemplation—the thought of things done.

June 15, 1888

The old woman is always the best woman, certain other things being equal.

August 5, 1888

Whitman about 1888. Charles E. Feinberg Collection

....

WORDS & LANGUAGE

....

Fire burned cheerfully in stove—wood flaming up. W
looked fine—spruced: wore his dark gray pantaloons: clean
shirt, spotless ruffles folded back over the sleeves of his
coat: hair flowing: complexion pale pink . . . .

I found an old pamphlet nearly destroyed under W.'s
rocker. Picked it up. "What is it?" It proved to be a copy
of Democratic Vistas (edition 1871). W. said to me:
"Take it along—keep it: but why shouldn't you have another copy?—a perfect copy? It is changed, you will find,
in later editions." Then, however: "No—take this as a
curio: it is well to have that just as it is." Then wrote in
it with blue pencil: "Horace Traubel from Walt Whitman
Nov: 18 '88." . . . Allusion was made to two of the railroad stations in Germantown—Wingohocking, Tulpehoc-
ken. "They are beautiful names," said W.: "they should be
kept: they have some reasons for being." Again: "Why
should we give up the native for borrowed names? Down
in this country—right here, near us—there was a place
called Longacoming: the name was fine, fine—the mere
sound of it: yet they got it into their fat heads that the
name was not satisfactory: they met, put the old name aside
for a new name: changed Longacoming to Berlin: oh God!"

November 18, 1888

....

Ain't that a good word?—howdydo. It has a phonetic significance—has pith, is straight-to. I am told that in some places west the salutation is still further abbreviated. You meet a man: you ask, How?

August 19, 1888

. . . my word "Presidentiad." Oh! that is eminently a word to be cherished—adopted. Its allusion, the four years of the Presidency: its origin that of the Olympiad—but as I flatter myself, bravely appropriate, where not another one word, signifying the same thing, exists!

May 17, 1889

It's not quite the thing to take language by the throat and make it yield you beautiful results. I don't want beautiful results—I want results: honest results.

May 1, 1888

I know of nothing I think of so little account as pretty words, pretty thoughts, pretty china, pretty arrangements.

August 24, 1888

. . . my own defect is more in the direction of interpolation, interlineation—in the insertion of words: I am only slowly satisfied with my verbal achievements: I remake over and over, as you have seen.

March 8, 1889

I never knew any other language but the English. I never liked text books—could never study a foreign language. Did

I say I never knew any language but the English? My enemies would even dispute my knowledge of the English.

May 12, 1888

I can say I doubt the compatibility of a universal language—yet, I honor, respect, the ambition of those who
idealize about it. I am inclined to feel that it goes with
evolution, is incident to progress, that there should be different languages. . . . Language is a thing which takes its
own path of growth—may some day merge all tongues into
one tongue but will not do so by an edict of scholars or a
pronunciamento from the universities. A universal language
has a lot to provide for—must provide for the Asiatic and
the African as well as for us—must not cast out any nation, any people, however remote. I do not say a universal
language may not grow but I am sure it cannot be deliberately made piecemeal by scholastic machinery.

October 23, 1888

After all,—deducting for all charges against its music,
what-not—I should not wonder but the English tongue is
the richest in possibilities of expression—potential for the
most varied combinations, beauties, wonders, of speech!

September 7, 1889

I have never been translated into the French except in
bits. It is an interesting mystery to me, how I would pass
the ordeal of getting into another language. I shall never
know, of course: I know no language but my own.

May 8, 1888

. . . it sounded like a translation made by a man who started to translate the book before he had read it.

December 9, 1888

. . . in spite of the fact that he is a translator, [he] writes an English letter like an Irish Indian.

February 25, 1889

I get humors—they come over me—when I resent being discussed at all, whether for good or bad—almost resent the good more than the bad: such emotional revolts: against you all, against myself: against words—God damn them, words: even the words I myself utter: wondering if anything was ever done worth while except in the final silences.

January 23, 1889

THE WRITER

A couple of volumes of poetry from unknown writers reached W. by mail today. "Everybody is writing, writing, writing—worst of all, writing poetry. It'd be better if the whole tribe of the scribblers—every damned one of us— were sent off somewhere with toolchests to do some honest work."

April 17, 1888

. . . I in the main like traders, workers, anyone, better than authors. The author class is a priest class with esoteric doctrines: I do not easily mix with it—I refuse to condone it.

September 8, 1888

He has that flea in his head: he thinks he must write: enlighten the world.

January 10, 1889

I believe everybody I know writes books or something— everybody: some of them write everything—poetry, stories, essays, God knows what not. I believe if I met a man who had not written a book I should hug him—he would be a monumental exception—an honorable exception.

May 25, 1888

I reckon I was not made to understand the scribbling class—perhaps they were not made to understand me. We seem to have been made for different jobs. I am doing my job in my way: it don't suit them: they growl, curse, ridicule: but what is left for Walt Whitman to do but complete the job in the most workmanlike fashion he knows?

April 19, 1888

I was . . . full of designs for things that were never executed: lectures, songs, poems, aphorisms, plays—why, even stories: I was going to write stories, too, God help me! It took me some time to get down, or up, to my proper measure—to take my own measure—that is, a long time to really get started—though I think that after I had made up my mind and got going I kept up a pretty steady pace in that one direction.

July 14, 1888

I used to have trouble with myself about the dignity of authors—whether it comported well with the rest of him that an author should peddle his own books. I got bravely over all doubts on that point. My theory is that the author might be the maker even of the body of his book—set the type, print the book on a press, put a cover on it, all with his own hands: learning his trade from A to Z—all there is of it. The literary craftsman should not be so helpless with his hands.

October 14, 1888

. . . a writer, to reflect life, nature—be true to himself, to his art (if we may say that)—must throw identity, over-mastering identity, personality, verve, into his pages.

October 26, 1888

A writer can do nothing for men more necessary, satisfying, than just simply to reveal to them the infinite possibilities of their own souls.

November 21, 1888

I take it there are qualities—latent forces—in all men which need to be shaken up into life: to shake them up— that is the function of the writer.

November 21, 1888

So many of the fellows do go all right for awhile then suddenly stop—are arrested—develop no further—or go back, retreat: so many of them: the brilliant men particularly: those who have no faith—who have only cleverness: the smart fellows, the gaudy glittering showy men and women whose main idea in writing is to surprise, startle, transfix, the reader, instead of filtering into people gradually, subtly, by the mere force, vehemence, of an exalted faith.

January 1, 1889

It is wonderful how much of one's manuscript a few compact pages of type will chaw up—consume—do away with: sometimes it is a terrible astonishment and ordeal for a poor writer to go through.

July 1, 1889

. . . most authors have the same dread—the dread that something or other essential that they have written may somehow become side-tracked, lost—lost forever.

May 16, 1888

WRITING

W. said as I was going: "I am watching your pieces as they appear in the papers and magazines. . . . I don't seem to have any advice to give, except perhaps this: Be natural, be natural, be natural! Be a damned fool, be wise if you must (can't help it), be anything—only be natural! Almost any writer who is willing to be himself will amount to something—because we all amount to something, to about the same thing, at the roots. The trouble mostly is that writers become writers and cease to be men: writers reflect writers, writers again reflect writers, until the man is worn thin—worn through."

May 22, 1888

··················

Above all, write your own way: don't take my word for anything—anyone's word—just take your own; follow your own intuition about it all, feeling sure that in the long run no other guide can lead you so surely to the truth.

June 15, 1888

I am very notionate, particular, about quotations: I never lug them in: if they don't come naturally by their place—fit to the last angle—then I reject them.

May 29, 1889

Quoting is a thing that gets to be a disease.

November 17, 1888

The best writing has no lace on its sleeves.

June 23, 1888

I care little for a man's means so the end comes around in its time. . . . the point is, not to prove your possession of a style, but to move the people along the line of their nobler impulses. The style will readily enough accommodate itself.

July 20, 1888

. . . the secret of it all, is to write in the gush, the throb, the flood, of the moment—to put things down without deliberation—without worrying about their style—without waiting for a fit time or place. I always worked that way. I took the first scrap of paper, the first doorstep, the first desk, and wrote—wrote, wrote. No prepared picture, no elaborated poem, no after-narrative could be what the thing itself is. You want to catch its first spirit—to tally its birth. By writing at the instant the very heart-beat of life is caught.

July 22, 1888

Watch yourself closely. Make a habit of noting things you see—buildings, people, the crowds you face, stands,—touch off the fakirs along the busy ways—fear nothing except to overstep the truth. It would be a good thing to do if only for exercise, but you will do it for more than that.

May 4, 1889

Every literary fellow, artist—every man who has a big job of work to do—should have his own den—a coop entirely his own—with a cot in it, if need be, and a stove: a studio with a human side to it.

September 6, 1888

I have had people say to me: "Walt, you write as if it was no effort whatever for you to do so." That may be how it looks but that's not how it is.

January 27, 1889

My effort has always been to pack, condense, solidify—to get my material into the smallest space compatible with decency.

June 3, 1889

. . . I hate commas in wrong places.

January 22, 1889

For myself I have never had any difficulty in deciding what I should say and not say. First of all comes sincerity —frankness, open-mindedness: that is the preliminary: to talk straight out.

November 8, 1888

My rule has been, so far as I could have any rule (I could have no cast-iron rule)—my rule has been, to write what I have to say the best way I can—then lay it aside—taking it up again after some time and reading it afresh—the mind new to it. If there's no jar in the new reading, well and good—that's sufficient for me.

October 16, 1888

I rely a good deal upon my general feeling about a piece when it comes back to me in type.

July 24, 1888

I find myself much better able to appreciate a piece if I put it aside for a time after it is written—for months, even years: returning to it with a fresh spirit.

July 15, 1888

In most of us I think writing gets to be a disease. We scribble, scribble, scribble—eternally scribble: God looks on—it turns his stomach: and while we scribble we neglect life.

June 18, 1888

This photograph by Thomas Eakins, 1891, is perhaps the last picture of Whitman. He was 72. Charles E. Feinberg Collection

PERSONS MENTIONED

John White Alexander (1856–1915), artist, painter, enjoyed an immense vogue in his day. His painting of Whitman can be seen in the Metropolitan Museum of Art, New York.

Henry Bilstein & Son, Philadelphia, engravers and printers.

William Cullen Bryant (1794–1878), poet, lawyer, editor, critic, won early fame with "Thanatopsis," and "To a Waterfowl."

Richard Maurice Bucke (1837–1902), born in England, physician at the Asylum for the Insane, London, Ontario, Canada. He first met Whitman in Camden, became a close friend, faithful correspondent, and one of his literary executors. Author of *Walt Whitman,* 1883, *Walt Whitman, Man and Poet,* 1897; also, *Man's Moral Nature,* and *Cosmic Consciousness.*

John Burroughs (1837–1921), naturalist and author, met Whitman in Washington, where he, like Whitman, worked as a government clerk. With help from Whitman and William Douglas O'Connor, he wrote the first study of Whitman, *Notes on Walt Whitman as Poet and Person,* 1867.

J. Leonard Corning, Unitarian minister, Traubel's friend.

Mary Oakes Davis (c. 1838–1908), shared Whitman's house during his last seven years; heroine of *Walt Whitman in Mickle Street* by Elizabeth Leavitt Keller, 1921.

Thomas Donaldson, lawyer, author of *Walt Whitman the Man,* 1896, knew Whitman for sixteen years. Whitman remembered him in his will. "I give to Thomas Donaldson the big arm chair presented to me [by] his children."

Peter Doyle (b. 1847 in Ireland), former Confederate soldier from Alexandria, Virginia, horsecar conductor, seems to have been the closest of Whitman's younger friends in his Washington years. Letters written by Whitman to Doyle were published under the title, *Calamus,* edited by Richard Maurice Bucke, M.D., 1897.

Thomas Eakins (1844–1916), painter, sculptor, photographer, teacher, born in Philadelphia, worked and died in his native city. His portrait of Whitman is in the Pennsylvania Academy of the Fine Arts, Philadelphia.

George S. Ferguson of George S. Ferguson Company, printers and electrotypers, 15 North Seventh Street, Philadelphia.

Thomas Biggs Harned (1851–1921), lawyer, married Horace Traubel's sister Augusta. The Harneds were generous friends of Whitman's; he had many a Sunday dinner with them at their house on Federal Street, Camden. One of Whitman's literary executors, Harned edited several volumes of Whitmaniana.

William Sloane Kennedy (1850–1929), biographer, anthologist, wrote *Reminiscences of Walt Whitman,* 1896,

*The Fight of a Book for the World: A Companion Volume
to Leaves of Grass,* 1926, and edited *Walt Whitman's
Diary in Canada,* 1904.

Morris Lychenheim, a friend of Traubel's, was also a
brother-in-law.

David McKay (1860–1918), founder of David McKay
Company, publishers, Philadelphia, began his career by pub-
lishing an edition of *Leaves of Grass* rejected by James R.
Osgood & Co., Boston.

Anne Montgomerie (d. 1953, age 90) married Traubel
in 1891. She compiled *A Little Book of Nature Thoughts,*
1906—selected from Whitman's writings.

Harrison S. Morris (1856–1948), editor, poet, author
of *Walt Whitman, A Brief Biography with Reminiscences,*
1929. Morris dedicated his book "To the Memory of
Horace Traubel."

Sidney H. Morse's plaster bust of Whitman can be seen
in the Walt Whitman House, Camden. Whitman's estimate
of him: "If Morse had got a better start in sculpture he'd
have been the high jinks in the business: now he only kind
of hangs around the edge. He has the capacity—all capaci-
ties but one, I might say: he is not quite steady enough at
one thing ever to get the best out of it. He writes well—very
well—but don't write best: he speaks well—very well—but
don't speak best: and so with sculpture—his trade: he
models well—very well—but just misses modeling *best.* He
gets around about too much as my dear mother used to say
—don't root anywhere long enough to grow." WWWC, II.
388.

Musgrove. "There is to be a change of nurses tomorrow," Traubel wrote 14 July 1888. "Baker will go. A man named Musgrove will take his place—an older man."

William Douglas O'Connor (1832–1889), journalist, civil servant, author, born in Boston of Irish stock. When Whitman was dismissed from his post in the Department of the Interior, the summer of 1865, because he had written a book, *Leaves of Grass,* deemed obscene by the Secretary, O'Connor sprang to Whitman's defense with *The Good Gray Poet: A Vindication.* O'Connor's title became Whitman's sobriquet. In a preface to O'Connor's posthumous book, *Three Tales,* 1892, Whitman described him as "personally and intellectually the most attractive man I had ever met."

Frederick John Martin Oldach (1823–1907), German born and trained bookbinder, founder of Oldach Company, 1215 Filbert Street, Philadelphia.

William Osler, M.D. (1849–1919), born and educated in Canada, moved to Philadelphia in 1884, from there to Johns Hopkins Hospital and Medical School, Baltimore. In 1905 he went to Oxford, England. A famous physician and prolific writer on medical subjects, he was knighted by King George V.

Ernest Percival Rhys (1859–1946), English poet, critic, editor, edited Everyman's Library.

George Ripley (1802–1880), born in Greenfield, Massachusetts, Unitarian minister, reformer, writer, editor, president of Brook Farm, book reviewer of the *New York Tribune,* 1849 to 1880.

William Michael Rossetti (1829–1919), English author, poet, art critic, public servant, brother of Dante Gabriel Rossetti, and Christina Georgina Rossetti; his selection from *Leaves of Grass* titled *Poems of Walt Whitman,* 1868, with introduction by himself, won Whitman an English following.

John Swinton (1829–1901), born in Scotland, social reformer, editor with the *New York Times, New York Sun,* and founder, 1883, of *John Swinton's Paper.*

John Addington Symonds (1840–1893), English poet, author, translator, and university man.

George Washington Whitman (1829–1901) was ten years younger than his brother Walt. Walt named George's wife, Louisa Orr Haslam Whitman (1842–1892), executrix of his will.

Jeff Whitman (1833–1890), whose name was Thomas Jefferson Whitman, a surveyor and civil engineer, is said to have been Walt's favorite brother. Jeff accompanied him to New Orleans in 1848.

Ed Wilkins, Whitman's attendant from November 1888 to October 1889, sent by Dr. Bucke from Canada.

ABOUT THE AUTHOR

Walter Teller, who has a bachelor's degree from Haverford College and a Ph.D from Columbia University, was a Guggenheim fellow in 1953. He is the author of six books as well as coauthor or editor of others. His essays have appeared in the *New York Times Book Review*, the *American Scholar*, and other journals.

The text of this book was set in Caslon Linotype and printed by Offset on P & S Special Book manufactured by P. H. Glatfelter Co., Spring Grove, Pa. Composed, printed and bound by Quinn & Boden Company, Inc., Rahway, N.J.